Japan's Rise
to International
Responsibilities

Japan's Rise to International Responsibilities

The Case of Arms Control

REINHARD DRIFTE

THE ATHLONE PRESS
London and Atlantic Highlands, NJ

First published 1990 by The Athlone Press Ltd
1 Park Drive, London NW11 7SG
and 171 First Avenue, Atlantic Highlands, NJ 07716
© Professor Reinhard Drifte 1990

British Library Cataloguing in Publication Data
Drifte, Reinhard, *1951–*
    Japan's rise to international responsibilities: the case
    of arms control.
    1. Japan. Arms control
    I. Title
    327.1'74'0952

    ISBN 0-485-11385-6
    ISBN 0-485-12073-9 pbk

Library of Congress Cataloging in Publication Data
Drifte, Reinhard.
    Japan's rise to international responsibilities : the case of arms
    control / Reinhard Drifte.
        p. cm.
    Includes bibliographical references.
    ISBN 0-485-11385-6. — ISBN 0-485-12073-9 (pbk.)
    1. Arms control. 2. Japan—Military relations. I. Title.
JX1974.D78   1990
327.1'74'0952—dc20

Typeset by TJB Photosetting Ltd, Grantham, Lincolnshire
Printed in Great Britain by Billings, Worcester

To Collette

Contents

Abbreviations

ACDA	Arms Control and Disarmament Agency (Washington)
ASDF	Air Self Defence Force
ASEAN	Association of South East Asian Nations
ATR	Advanced Thermal Reactor
ASW	Anti-Submarine Warfare
CBM	Confidence-Building Measures
CD	Conference on Disarmament (Geneva)
CFRP	Carbon fibre reinforced plastics
CNS	Comprehensive national security
COCOM	Coordinating Committee for Multilateral Export Controls
CSCE	Conference on Security and Cooperation in Europe
CTB	Comprehensive (Nuclear) Test Ban
DA	Defence Agency (Japan)
DMZ	Demilitarized Zone
DOD	US Department of Defense
FBR	Fast Breeder Reactor
FLIR	Flight information region
FY	Fiscal Year
GSDF	Ground Self Defence Force

GLCM	Ground-launched Cruise Missile
IAEA	International Atomic Energy Agency
IISS	International Institute for Strategic Studies
INF	Intermediate range nuclear forces
INFCE	International Nuclear Fuel Cycle Evaluation
JCP	Japanese Communist Party
JSP	Japanese Socialist Party
LRINF	Long-range intermediate nuclear forces
MITI	Ministry of Trade and Industry
NASA	National Space Development Agency
NPT	Non-Proliferation Treaty
NRC	National Regulatory Commission
PKO	Peace-Keeping Operation
RIPS	Research Institute for Peace and Security (Tokyo)
RS	Remote-sensing satellite
SDF	Self Defence Forces
SDI	Strategic Defence Initiative
SIPRI	Stockholm International Peace Research Institute
SRINF	Short range intermediate nuclear forces
START	Strategic arms reduction talks
UN	United Nations

Foreword

This book has come into being as part of a major research project on 'High technology and Japan's defence' which the author started when he was Assistant Director of the International Institute of Strategic Studies. In the course of writing, the arms control module became too detailed to be fitted into the original book project.

The author owes particular thanks to Col John Cross, the Deputy Director of the IISS, for having given a thorough editorial sweep to an earlier version of the manuscript when it was still planned as part of the original book project. Thanks go also to J.A. Paleit, Director with Urenco in Marlow, for giving technical advice on the non-nuclear proliferation chapter. I would like to thank also several Japanese specialists for giving valuable comments on parts of the manuscript. All responsibility for the contents lies, of course, with me.

Introduction

Since the 1970s Japan has been faced with demands from its
allies, notably the US, to assume more responsibilities for
the support of the international system on which Japan's
success in achieving first economic and now financial superpower status is based. These responsibilities have mostly
been defined in terms of more military efforts and increased
contributions to the Third World. Arms control was, however, not included since it has been considered the domain of
the superpowers or at most a concern of the European countries. Moreover, it has been considered a complicating factor in fostering the general support of public opinion for
more defence efforts. In addition, the Japanese government
hardly saw vital national interests at stake. Intellectuals are
not attracted by the subject since their interest focuses on the
normative discourse of disarmament. Accepting arms control as a means to achieve a safer level of armament would
have meant acceptance of deterrence which is still abhorred
by the majority of Japanese scholars.

Japan's growing stakes as a member of the West and as a
technological superpower has gradually changed the country's position towards arms control, although this is realized
by only a few people inside and outside Japan. An advanced

technological power like Japan cannot afford to be removed from arms control and disarmament issues because international negotiations in this field have a bearing on its industrial, commercial and technological interests. The best example is the Non-Proliferation Treaty (NPT) and subsequent non-proliferation efforts which relate to all these three areas. In the case of the INF issue, Japan for the first time contributed to a successfully concluded superpower arms control agreement. In small part due to Japan's insistence, the Soviet Union finally gave up its original stance of leaving some INF weapons in Asia.

Because of its growing political and military significance on a regional and global level, the country's position on arms control and disarmament matters is becoming an important element in regional and global arms control and disarmament efforts. Arms control proposals for the Pacific have in recent years been promoted by the Soviet Union. However, any kind of arms control regime which has an effect on Japan's security or economic interests will increasingly need Tokyo's support if it is to be meaningful. In addition, Japan's technological power may lead to demands by other countries that Tokyo make some concrete contribution to certain arms control regimes. The 1987 agreement of the seven summit nations on the control of certain kinds of missiles is one illustration of Japan's possible future role in arms control as a result of its technological capability. Finally, it is also conceivable that Japan's growing military capabilities and its integration into the global American military posture may soon prompt some of its worried neighbours to ask Japan for arms control-related measures in order to remove suspicions about its ultimate motives.

This book is primarily concerned with arms control, although public debate in Japan, as will be explained later, is more centred on disarmament without being clear about the distinction between the two. Disarmament is understood in this book as the reduction or abolition of armaments; it can be multilateral or unilateral; general or local; comprehensive or partial; controlled or uncontrolled. Arms control does not aim primarily at the abolition of arms, since proponents of arms control consider the risk of war to be induced more by conflicts of interests than by weapons. Its major concern is the creation of stability, which means control of a dynamic process and not of a static situation.[1]

This book will deal with the place of arms control and disarmament in Japan's foreign and defence policies in a comprehensive way, that is, on a national, regional and global level. It will also analyse the institutional structure of the issue, the role of the public, and the function of economic and security interests in policy-making.[2] Based on an evaluation of these factors, the book will offer some conclusions on what contribution in the field of arms control can be expected from Japan.

CHAPTER I

The basis of arms control and disarmament politics in Japan

The international community started to link Japan with issues of arms control and disarmament when the INF debate spread from Europe to east Asia in the beginning of the 1980s. At that time, Japan began to voice concern about the then-proposed elimination of INF only in Europe. However, Japan had already played a considerable role in global arms control in the context of the Non-Proliferation Treaty (NPT) in the 1970s. It had also been active in technical discussions of the Conference on Disarmament (CD) in Geneva on issues such as the draft treaty on chemical weapons. Japan's technological expertise has also become a critical element for the successful regulation of a comprehensive nuclear test ban (CTB). On a regional level, Japan has contributed to stability by taking unilateral measures on a national level which have so far prevented it from becoming a military power commensurate with its economic power.[1] These measures, based on the war- and arms-renouncing Peace Constitution, can be called true national arms control and disarmament measures. They comprise:

1. The civilian control of the military establishment
2. The three non-nuclear principles

3. A ban on arms exports
4. A ban on sending military personnel for combat abroad
5. A ban on conscription
6. A ceiling on the defence budget of 1 per cent of the Gross National Product (GNP)
7. Commitment to the peaceful use of space.

Although these measures have a very high profile in Japanese domestic politics and have contributed to regional stability, they have not translated into a more active regional or global arms control and disarmament policy.

The discrepancy between a high profile arms control and disarmament policy on the national level and a very low profile arms control and disarmament policy on the regional and global level lies in the dichotomy within Japan's foreign and defence policy. Its unilateral arms control and disarmament measures were primarily designed by the government to bridge the gap between the political streams of the Peace Constitution of 1947 and the Japanese-American security alliance. As a result of this dichotomy, Japan's unilateral arms control and disarmament measures, based on the government's interpretation of the so-called Peace Constitution, have always been at variance with the security policies deriving from the Japanese-American security treaty.

In the Constitution of 1947, with its pacifist preamble and Article 9, Japan renounces for ever the right of belligerency and the right to maintain any sort of military force, putting its trust in the peace-loving peoples of the world. This was a reflection not only of the mood of the majority of the populace but also of the disarmed state of the country and the need to re-establish its reputation in the world.[2] Since then, the interpretation of the Constitution has been permanently changed in order better to match the conservative government's perceived need for Japan's own defence efforts as well as to accommodate American demands for a greater Japanese military role. As a result, the Constitution has changed from a kind of legal charter of complete disarmament to one which merely limits the scope and effectiveness of the post-war Japanese military establishment.

The tension between Japan's Peace Constitution and its security alliance with the US has resulted in its arms control and disarmament policy being relegated to domestic politics and never being integrated into Japan's defence policy. This has had a decisive influence on the conceptual framework of arms control and disarmament politics and its institutional foundations in Japan.

Arms control and disarmament and Japanese security policy

Rather than integrating arms control and disarmament into the country's security policy, the government has had to be careful that the contradictions inherent in some of its domestically orientated arms control measures, such as the three non- nuclear principles which clash with Japan's desire to be protected by the American nuclear umbrella, do not undermine its credibility. Against the background of changes in the strategic environment – the relative weakening of the United States and the political and economic upsurge of Japan – upholding unilateral arms control measures has become even more difficult. The government has been able to work around the three non-nuclear principles, narrow down the ban on arms exports by allowing arms technology export to the US and abolishing the 1 per cent ceiling on defence spending. Increasingly committed to expanding Japan's military capabilities, the government has become ever more suspicious of arms control as it relates to Japan, since it could jeopardize the growing consensus on greater Japanese defence efforts. Since the accession to power of the Suzuki Cabinet in 1980, the Japanese government has publicly espoused the concept of the balance of power in order to justify increased defence efforts. After former Prime Minister Suzuki had also emphasized it in his speech to the UN Special Session on Disarmament in 1982, the *New York Times* interpreted the speech as a curtain-raiser for a policy of increased Japanese defence efforts.[3] But the government has now also begun to recognize that 'disarmament and national security are two sides of the same coin'.[4]

The weakness of Japan's arms control and disarmament policies is also linked to a lack of awareness on the part of Japan's policy-makers of the interrelationship between state-of-the-art military technology and many of their arms control policies. In the cautiously phrased words of Imai Ryukichi, Japan's former disarmament ambassador in Geneva:

> Since Japan has not been very deeply involved in the most advanced of post-war military technologies, there have also been possibilities that her position regarding arms control may have been out of phase with some of the military realities. There are some rather delicate problems in terms of nuclear explosive testing, or targeting of long-range missiles over the arctic region, or capabilities to pin-point incoming re-entry vehicles, which may have serious influences on arms control measures, which, however, are not part of the common knowledge. It is, therefore, sometimes not very comfortable to pursue traditional and some-what declaratory approaches to arms control and dis-armament without comprehension as to the basic technologies of the problem.... Deeper involvement in the basic research by those qualified and willing throughout the world might give them benefit of becoming more sensitive to the realities of the politics of science and technology of the world.[5]

However, changes in the regional strategic environment in recent years have advanced not only the popular consensus on increased self-defence efforts, but also Japanese perspectives on the necessity for arms control and its place in Japan's security policy. While the unilateral limitations on Japan's armed forces and other related measures are interpreted in a more relaxed fashion, arms control issues can no longer be considered the domain of only the superpowers or the UN.

Japan, like other Asian countries, cannot afford to ignore the prospect of reduced tensions in Europe, supported by Confidence-Building Measures (CBM) and arms control agreements such as the INF agreement of December 1987 or the 50 per cent cut in strategic weapons planned by the two superpowers. Such a situation could give the US and the Soviet Union a freer hand in the Asia-Pacific region and provide an incentive for Japan and other Asian countries to re-evaluate the merits of arms control in their own region.[6] Recent Soviet arms reduction proposals will enhance pressure on the American administration to reduce its overseas military deployment in Asia since it has to cut military expenditures in view of the budget deficit.

Japan has become heavily involved in the INF issue less for reasons of national security interests than in order to achieve equality in the western camp. The issue of the reduction of nuclear weapons, which has become more pertinent since the Reykjavik Summit in November 1986, has increased concern in the Japanese government about the reliability of the American nuclear umbrella. Co-operation on arms control issues has therefore become one of the key symbols of the closer, more consultative character of the Japan- US relationship demanded by some in the Japanese government. Foreign Minister Kuranari declared in April 1987 before the Japanese-American Shimoda Conference:

This issue (of nuclear arms reduction) would require Japan-US policy co-ordination on a wide spectrum of problems: This includes those in the military areas

[such] as the maintenance of credibility of the extended nuclear deterrence provided through the Japan-US security arrangements, the promotion of Japan-US defence co-operation and the further strengthening of Japan's self-defence capabilities. It also involves those in the political fields such as securing Western solidarity to support the US in its negotiations with the Soviets and further includes those which involve economic aspects of controlling technology transfer to the Soviets. This issue also includes questions requiring co-ordination between Japan and West Europe as is demonstrated in the case of the INF.[7]

Another area where Japanese political leaders want more arms control-related consultation with the US is the Korean peninsula where American policy could suddenly change dramatically as it did in the 1970s when Carter proposed the withdrawal of American ground troops. Budgetary constraints on the US, the growing economic and military strength of South Korea, economic frictions with South Korea and the diminished popular support of the Koreans for American troops in their country will probably lead to cuts of American military deployment in Korea.

Arms control in Asia could also help reduce tensions created by the linkage between global and regional military competitions. Some in Japan realize that Japan cannot just continue to rely solely on strengthening its armed forces and welcoming any American force enhancement in Asia without taking into consideration what the superpowers found out in the 1970s and 1980s: that an uncontrolled arms race does not increase security but rather diminishes it. This also seems to be gradually becoming recognized by military officers who have hitherto been most reluctant to consider the merits of arms control for Japan's security in view of the country's unilateral arms control measures. Col. Nakamura Yoshihisa was probably the first active officer in the SDF to recognize publicly that arms control, in this case CBM, could play a positive role in Japan's security policy on a tactical and technical level and in this way increase the effectiveness of Japan's deterrence against the Soviet Union (see Chapter V)[8]

The institutional framework

A mechanism for addressing issues of arms control and disarmament was institutionally established in the governmental bureaucracy only after Japan became a member of the United Nations in 1956. In 1966 a disarmament room (*gunshuku shitsu*) was established within the UN Bureau of the Foreign Ministry, which was promoted to the level of division in April 1978. This reflected the perception that disarmament was to be considered merely a UN issue, not as something pertaining to Japan's security. In deference to UN parlance and the pacifist mood in Japan, the term 'disarmament' was used instead of the phrase 'arms control'.

The peace movement supported indirectly the government's lukewarm approach to arms control and disarmament. It shows little concern for the piecemeal approach of the UN's deliberations and instead indulges in general demands for total disarmament and ritual annual demonstrations in August. Acceptance of arms control as a means to create a more peaceful world would mean the acceptance of deterrence by military force, including nuclear weapons. The movement has also been weakened by fragmentation along party lines and the issuance of very general peace slogans in order to get the broadest support possible. This general lack of realism was encouraged by the perception that, until the 1970s, disarmament and arms control were clearly monopolized by the superpowers which focused on strategic nuclear matters.[9]

Unlike the Ministry of Foreign Affairs, the Defence

Agency (DA) has no arms control office. Events such as the INF negotiations, with their direct implications for Japan, have led to an increase in the DA's interest in arms control. Although the number of Foreign Ministry personnel dealing with arms control has increased in Tokyo as well as at Japan's delegation in Geneva, the site of the UN Conference on Disarmament, an arms control constituency has only recently begun to develop. In the Disarmament Division of the Foreign Ministry, there were (as of summer 1987) nine diplomats and four clerical staff. In addition, the division has had one member from the ASDF for the last ten years. The previous four division chiefs had all been either in the security or the Soviet Union division, an indication that the division is being given more importance in terms of Japan's security policy.[10] Within the last ten years Japan has been represented by excellent ambassadors at the CD. Imai Ryukichi, the ambassador from 1983 to 1986, has a background in engineering and nuclear physics and has himself drafted and tabled several working papers on technical issues, a rarity among CD ambassadors. His predecessor, Okawa Yoshio, whose involvement with arms control goes back to the handling of the NPT in the Diet in the 1970s, was a highly esteemed representative because of his diplomatic skill and his dedication to the pursuit of real progress within the CD.

There is still a lack of permanent and institutionalized links between the bureaucracy and outside institutions undertaking research on arms control and disarmament. Outsiders are consulted only on a case-by-case basis. This involves mainly technical issues on specific subjects, such as the planned convention on chemical weapons or seismic tests for a comprehensive nuclear test ban which are under negotiation in the CD in parallel with the superpowers' talks. The Disarmament Division has legal experts to consult on the issue of outer space and a specialist from the GSDF Chemical School to consult on chemical weapons.

Political and strategic consultations are very limited.

The main reason for the small community of arms control and disarmament specialists in a country with hundreds of universities and research institutes is that strategic and military matters have been until very recently taboo subjects. In this atmosphere arms control could not be regarded as a practical policy to enhance Japan's security. Involvement in arms control amounts to an acceptance that military power is an essential element of national security policy despite the explicit stipulation in the Peace Constitution. This is still a difficult proposition for most liberal and left-leaning academics who form the majority at Japan's universities. Even fewer would agree that arms control and nuclear deterrence are not mutually exclusive.

The number of institutions working on arms control and disarmament is slowly growing. The Japan Institute of International Affairs (*Nihon Kokusai Mondai Kenkyujo*), a research institution funded mainly by the Foreign Ministry, deals with arms control and disarmament issues. In 1985, a former professor of international relations, Prof. Maeda Hisashi, the doyen of academic research on arms control in Japan, established the Disarmament Research Institute. This, however, is still a very small operation, financed by the founder and its research is very limited. It publishes at irregular intervals a periodical called *Gendai no Gunshuku* (*Disarmament Today*). In September 1980, a member of the Upper House, Utsunomiya Tokuma, established a small institute, the Utsunomiya Disarmament Research Room (*Utsunomiya Gunshuku Kenkyushitsu*) which publishes a monthly bulletin (*Gunshuku Mondai Shiryo*). This organization is also funded by its founder. Several peace research centres attached to universities, such as Hiroshima University and Soka University, sometimes deal with arms control. The most important research institute for arms control and disarmament is the Tokyo-based Research Institute for Peace and Security (RIPS) which is funded by international foundations such as the Ford Foundation but also accepts money from the government. Its annual *Asian Security* has become a standard reference work for all who have a serious interest not only in security-related matters, but also in political and economic developments in countries ranging from south to north-east Asia. This annual always includes a chapter on arms control which gives an account of arms control developments as they relate to east Asia. The Institute was commissioned by the government to produce a study on confidence-building measures, carried out by academics from civilian universities as well as from the Defence University in Yokosuka.

CHAPTER II

Changes in Japan's national arms control measures

In response to demands from the US to shoulder more of its own as well as regional defence and faced with a growing Soviet military presence in east Asia, Japan's national arms control measures have been gradually relaxed. In December 1986, the government abandoned the 1 per cent ceiling on the size of the annual defence budget. The planned defence budget for FY 1989 is ¥3900 bn ($28.8 bn). This puts Japan in terms of spending roughly on a par with Great Britain which ranks third after the United States and the Soviet Union. However, if the defence budget is calculated according to NATO yardsticks, the Japanese defence expenditures in 1988 amounted to $41 bn, the third highest in the world. The steep appreciation of the yen has brought more purchasing power for the SDF which obtains its most sophisticated military equipment from the United States. As a result of its political will and economic strength, Japan has today a military capability which has to be rated first-class in regional as well as global terms. On the other hand, the dispatch of troops abroad is still not allowed under the SDF Law of 1954 (Article 3) which provides for the mobilization of troops solely in the case of external attack and violent unrest. There is no move by the government so far to revise this law. The overseas dispatch of the SDF is also prohibited by a June 1954 Diet resolution. Until recently the government did not even permit the dispatch of any personnel for UN Peace Keeping Operations (PKO). Of more immediate interest to the subject of this book is the softening of the ban on arms exports and the possible intrusion of military aspects into the peaceful use of space. A close look at these developments is useful because they will have a bearing on the extent and credibility of future Japanese contributions to arms control.

Tensions between alliance politics and the ban on arms exports

In the mid-1960s, Japan's arms exports increased sharply because of the government's co-operative attitude towards Japanese industry supplying the American forces in the Vietnam War. The war was, however, very unpopular in Japan, and there was an ever growing concern about possible Japanese involvement. As a result, in 1967 Prime Minister Sato announced three restrictions on arms exports, reinforcing rules which were already contained in the Export Trade Control Order of 1949. The new restrictions explicitly prohibited arms exports to Communist countries, countries subject to UN sanctions and parties to international disputes.[1] In February 1976, in response to concern raised by the disclosure of illegal arms sales, Prime Minister Miki's cabinet extended the ban to all other countries as well, and in addition prohibited the export of weapon-related technology and production equipment. These severe limitations were supported by a resolution of the Diet.

As a result, Japan officially does not export weapons and hence there are no official statistics available from Japan on this matter. The only source for such statistics is the annual publication *World Military Expenditures and Arms Transfers* produced by the Arms Control and Disarmament Agency

(ACDA) in Washington. The *Yearbook* of the Stockholm International Peace Research Institute ceased publishing such figures in 1977. According to ACDA, in 1985 Japan exported weapons valued at $90m. (current dollars).[2] However, it is not clear what ACDA's sources of information are or what items are considered as weapons.

Japan's apparently stringent ban has several loopholes. The role of high technology is the main factor which undermines the ban. According to the government's policy guidelines, the term 'weapon' refers to goods that are 'used by military forces and directly employed in combat'. This definition leaves open a large grey area, such as rolling stock, electronic equipment and machinery which are dual-purpose items and where the end-user determines whether or not the item is employed as a weapon. Hence, many items of Japanese origin have found their way into the armed forces of a number of countries. Kawasaki Heavy Industries V-107 helicopters have been sold to Swedish, Burmese and Saudi Arabian military and paramilitary forces. Over the period 1976–79 mortar barrels were sold to South Korea as semi-finished goods (*hanseihin*). The author has seen Japanese jeeps in the Nicaraguan army. Japan reportedly sold dual-purpose items such as transports and small boats to Iran.[3] When Chadian forces overran Libyan forces in March 1987, it was reported that they relied mainly on portable weapons and Toyota pick-up trucks.[4] In June 1987 the US informed Japan that North Korea had converted heavy-duty trucks, 156 of which had been imported from the Nissan Diesel Motor Corporation since 1978, into missile-launchers.[5]

The most important inroads into the ban on arms exports, however, arise out of the export of high-technology goods, principally electronics and electrical components. Almost half of Japan's electronics industry's production goes abroad and amounted in 1987 to $55 bn, after having surpassed automobiles as the largest single export category for the first time in 1984. The Japanese contribution of electronics technology and components to American weapon systems has become crucial. The same applies in varying degrees to the weapon systems of other countries.

The spirit of the arms export ban has also been undermined by the construction of military bases by Japanese companies in foreign countries, the exemption of procurement orders by the American forces in Japan from MITI approval and arms exports through joint production schemes and foreign subsidiaries.[6] The increasing number of Japanese companies either moving abroad or buying overseas production facilities because of the steep rise of the yen since 1985 will make control of the arms export ban even more illusory.

In the meantime, Japan's arms production capability is expanding with the steady increase of defence expenditures. More and more companies are joining the number of arms-related manufacturers. In FY 1988 the Defence Agency spent ¥10.3 trillion on equipment purchases compared with ¥3.2 trillion ten years before. This increases industrial pressure to abolish the ban on arms exports in order to enjoy economies of scale and win new markets.

The November 1983 agreement to permit sales of arms technology to the US was the first major official departure from the arms export ban. The growing interest of Japanese companies has increased the pressure on the government to do away with the ban altogether. But the business community is still far from being unanimous on this matter, and the following considerations will prevent an official abandonment of the present cabinet policy at least for the foreseeable future:

1. The opposition parties and a majority of the public are fundamentally opposed to arms exports. This opposition is not only an issue of moral principle, but stems from a public fear of becoming involved in international conflicts.

2. Arms exports would seriously interfere with Japan's traditional policy of pursuing good relations with as many countries as possible and of trying to prevent a situation where the government would be forced to take sides.

3. Japanese competition in the world arms market would increase trade frictions with Japan's western allies. These frictions and tensions are already high and protectionism is rising; any gain in arms sales would be likely to be offset by a surge in anti-Japanese protectionist measures.

4. The prices of Japanese weapons are too high. Increased sales figures cannot immediately change this handicap, especially in the case of major weapon systems such as tank and aircraft, which cannot be mass produced like automobiles or television.

5. It is very likely that Japanese arms exports on a large and open scale would mean an end of the present technology exchange regime not only with the US, but also with other foreign weapon producers. In addition, military product development is a voracious user of scarce scientific and technological resources, and the drain of such expertise at the expense of civilian product development would be felt very quickly.[7]

The peaceful use of space

In recent years Japan has made considerable advances in the development of launchers and satellites and in reducing its heavy dependence on American technology. All launchers used for Japanese-made satellites are manufactured in Japan and in the case of the most recent model, the H-1 with a lift capacity of 550 kg for geostationary satellites, 84 per cent is domestically produced. In the case of satellites, the Japanese have focused on earth observation and communications satellites which have the greatest commercial benefit. However, in the context of this book, such satellites are also relevant for military as well as specific arms control purposes. In February 1987 Japan launched its Momo-1 earth observation satellite. It has a resolution of 50m, which is not as good as the earlier Soviet, US Landsat and French SPOT systems but it is comparable to India's remote-sensing satellite (RRS). However, it is the first satellite to gather data on sea, land and atmosphere simultaneously, using three different sensors.[8] In September 1988 Japan launched, with Sakura 3b, its latest communication satellite, capable of handling 6000 telephone circuits.

The Diet resolution of 9 May 1969 limits the utilization of space to peaceful purposes. Japan is also a signatory to the Outer Space and Celestial Bodies Treaty which prohibits the placing of nuclear weapons or any other weapons of mass destruction in orbit around the earth or on any celestial body other than the earth. The Diet resolution is very explicit:

> The development and exploitation by Japan of objects to be projected into space above the earth's atmosphere, and of the rockets by which they are launched shall be confined to peaceful purposes only and shall be carried out to contribute to the purpose of science, the improvement of the nation's living standards, and the welfare of human society, along with the development of industrial technology and voluntary international collaboration and cooperation.[9]

With the great advances in Japanese launcher and satellite technology and the availability of international satellite services for communications and observation, as well as growing integration and co-operation with the US forces, the government found it necessary to weaken the resolution's stress on peaceful (i.e. non-military) uses of space. In a government guideline in February 1985, two approaches were adopted to allow the use of satellites for the SDF. One was to make a distinction between lethal and non-lethal uses of satellites and the other to exempt dual-purpose satellites, thus applying the same interpretation technique as has been used to weaken the ban on arms exports. In the words of the guidelines:

> 1. Clearly, the wording 'for peaceful purposes only,' used in the resolution, signified disapproval of direct use by the SDF of any satellite as a lethal or destructive weapon. The government interprets the Diet resolution as prohibiting the SDF from exploiting any satellite unless it is commonly used. Accordingly, the government considers that the SDF may be permitted to use any satellite which is in common use and any other satellite which is capable of similar functions.
> 2. The Fleetsat satellite, which was discussed in the Diet, is a telecommunications satellite used by the US for military purposes, but this satellite is capable of the same functions as other satellites which are now commonly used, such as Intelsat, Inmalsat and CS-2 (Sakura No. 2). Therefore, the government does not hold that the use of the Fleetsat satellite by the SDF runs counter to the meaning of the Diet resolution in its approval of space development and exploitation for 'peaceful purposes only'.[10]

The practical consequences of this reinterpretation had actually already begun in 1985 when the government approved SDF use of the Sakura No. 2 communication satellite for radio transmissions between the mainland and a base on the Ogasawara islands.[11] In FY 1985, the DA appropriated ¥168 million ($704,284, $1=¥238.54) to equip five escort ships with equipment to monitor data from the US Navy's Fleetsat communications system.[12] It was also reported that Japan had been collecting intelligence via Landsat since March 1985 and that the government intended to purchase data from the French SPOT satellite for the

Defence Agency.[13] In 1986 it became known that Space Communications Corporation, a Mitsubishi-affiliated satellite communications company, would build a communications system to link major SDF bases and stations by utilizing ComSat 'Super Bird', to be launched in 1988.[14]

The Diet resolution on the utilization of space has also played an important role in the attacks by the opposition on SDI and the question of Japanese participation. The government's view has been, however, that the resolution refers only to Japan's own activities and within Japanese territory and does not cover projects initiated by another country.[15] In July 1987, however, Mitsubishi Heavy Industries declined the request by McDonnell-Douglas for the transfer of the technology of the domestically developed LE-5 rocket engine because of the possibility that it might be used for launching American military satellites. The American company planned to use the Japanese engine as the second stage of its Delta rocket which had gained increased importance because of the lack of US space launch capability following the Challenger disaster.[16] The Japanese refusal was probably motivated by commercial concerns because Mitsubishi Heavy Industries is very interested in SDI.

Another test for the application of the space resolution is likely to arise from Japan's participation in the multilateral space station programme. Although it was originally planned by the US, western Europe and Japan as a civilian project, the Pentagon has started to seek use of the space station for some military purposes. In February 1987, James Fletcher, the head of NASA, told the US Congressional Committee on Science, Space and Technology that NASA had reached agreement with DOD permitting fundamental research aboard the space station but prohibiting the installation of weapon systems. In the same month, in multilateral talks in Washington, the US said it would give priority to its own national interests in deciding how to use the planned space station. In April 1987 it was reported that the Pentagon and American industry were examining plans to use the American module of the multilateral space station for the repair and refuelling of military-related space facilities. The next generation of American intelligence-gathering satellites will have its engines refuelled by astronauts working from either the space shuttles or the space station in order to enhance the usefulness of these satellites.[17] The same month, in an official letter, then US Defence Secretary Weinberger urged the military use of the space station and warned against putting too much emphasis on a multi-national effort if this would endanger US strategic interests. He also warned against the US losing control over its technology.[18] The Science and Technology Agency, which is in charge of Japan's participation in the space station, is particularly wary of becoming involved in military-related projects and was apparently shocked by this American insistence. On the other hand, one Japanese news-paper report described the Ministry of Foreign Affairs as having declared that DOD's future activity aboard the base would not conflict with Japan's space development policy provided the activities did not exceed the fundamental research phase as indicated in the earlier statement by the NASA Director.[19] Japan is very interested in participating in this multinational venture which exceeds the present scope of its own technology, and has already invested some funds. 1986 and 1987 saw many bilateral and multilateral rounds of talks aimed at concluding a final agreement to replace pre-sent agreements (Phase A and Phase B agreements) under the Science and Technology Agreement which cover only the feasibility and design work of the space lab.[20] In the summer of 1987 the US administration tabled a draft treaty calling for the civilian and peaceful use of the space station, while stipulating that the adjective 'peaceful' does not pre-clude use for national security purposes.[21] However, the Japanese define 'peaceful' as 'non-military' (*higunji*). The compromise reached during the seventh round of the

Japanese-American space station negotiations in August 1987 was that the Japanese module alone would be bound by the principles of the Japanese space regulations.[22] The final agreement reached in February 1988 by all participating nations followed these lines. Each nation will operate according to its national principles and will have the right to refuse the military-related use of its material contribution.[23] In this respect Japan has found common ground with participating West European countries who also seek to avoid involvement in a space venture with significant military overtones.

The nuclear umbrella and the three non-nuclear principles

One of the bedrock elements of the Japanese-American security treaty system is the deterrence provided by the American commitment to the defence of Japan not only with conventional but also with nuclear weapons. Successive Japanese governments have worked hard on their American ally to maintain this commitment, which was first made in the Japan-US joint statement of 1965 between former Prime Minister Sato and President Johnson. The American side promised to defend Japan against any military attack, including by nuclear weapons. When Nakasone visited the US in 1970 as Director General of the Defence Agency, he solicited from then Secretary of Defense Laird a renewed promise that the US would defend Japan 'by all means'.[24] Clearly the US can provide this nuclear deterrence only if it has military forces with nuclear weapons in Asia. Of course, these weapons in Asia serve to underpin not only Japanese security but also that of other allied countries in the Asia-Pacific region. Nevertheless, Japan has been playing a crucial role in American nuclear strategy since the deployment of nuclear weapons in the Far East in the 1950s.[25]

As it is the only country to have suffered the effects of nuclear bombing, Japan's post-war pacifism has become synonymous with nuclear allergy. From the outset, the conservative government has therefore faced widespread opposition to the nuclear component of the Japanese-American security treaty. Following controversies involving the access of nuclear-powered units of the US Seventh Fleet to Japanese harbours, then Prime Minister Sato, in December 1967, enunciated his three non-nuclear principles which remain the official basis of Japan's nuclear policy. The principles, which are backed by a Diet resolution, provide that Japan will neither possess, nor manufacture, nor permit entry of nuclear weapons into the country.[26] The domestic origin of the three non-nuclear principles led Kosaka Masataka, a prominent defence specialist, to write:

> Japan should not be too proud of its position on nuclear weapons, for its policies were not created intentionally; Japan's security policy was born out of necessity and has developed through the interaction of opposing points of view. It is, in a word, an accidental product of circumstances and politics.[27]

Opposition forces in Japan have for many years pointed at the alleged contradiction between the Japanese-American security treaty and its day-to-day practical manifestations on the one hand and the three non-nuclear principles on the other (in 1985 at least thirty-two nuclear submarines called at Yokosuka and Sasebo).[28] The government has so far stuck to its official policy that no nuclear weapons can be brought into Japan. Under the Japanese–American security treaty the introduction of such weapons could only follow consultations, and the government declares that it would invariably turn down such requests by the US, even in the case of an emergency. However, there have been at least two occasions on which a prime minister has stated that in an emergency, American nuclear weapons might be permitted. However, both statements have subsequently been withdrawn in the face of uproar from the opposition and the media.[29]

The government insists on its three non-nuclear principles despite a series of revelations of violations of the third principle. In 1974, the *New York Times* reported that there had been an agreement in 1960, permitting the introduction of nuclear weapons by ship or aircraft but that the Japanese had deliberately not retained a written text so as to be able to deny the agreement. In January 1975 a former American admiral, Gene Laroque, declared that some American warships carried nuclear weapons on board when they entered Japanese harbours. In 1981 Professor Reischauer, US ambassador to Japan from 1961 to 1966, confirmed this statement as did other former officials in Japan and the US. The gist of the statements was to confirm the 1974 *New York Times* report that the Japanese government had in 1960 secretly agreed that an earlier explicit Japanese non-nuclear stance preliminary to Sato's pronouncement (i.e. the Atomic Energy Basic Act of December 1955) did not include their transit, and did not even necessitate prior consultations under the clause of the Japanese-American security treaty which makes such consultations mandatory in case of major shifts in the American military deployment in Japan.[30]

In 1987 a Japanese Communist Party (JCP) member found in the US Library of Congress a recently declassified 1966 telegram from then Secretary of State Dean Rusk to the US Embassy in Tokyo stating that if a nuclear-free zone proposal then being pressed by the Soviets was accepted by Japan, 'it is possible that the ambiguity [Japan] has accepted on [the] presence of nuclear weapons on US vessels in Japanese ports and on transiting US aircraft might no longer be accepted'. The telegram also referred to a 'confidential 1960 agreement' governing such matters.[31] Neither the Japanese nor the American government contested the authenticity of the Rusk cable, but both tried denying the existence of a secret agreement in 1960. During the ensuing Diet discussions, the JCP also provided oral testimony from a former Department of Defence official who confirmed having seen the 1960 agreement.[32] In the summer of 1987 the Japanese news agency Kyodo reported the discovery of a May 1984 instruction by the Commander-in-Chief of the US Pacific Forces instructing regional military commanders in several Pacific nations, including Japan, to work out plans to control nuclear accidents or incidents and to try to present them as conventional accidents or incidents.[33] Despite all these reports, the American side refuses to comment on the presence of nuclear weapons while, for its part, the Japanese government declares its faith in American respect for the three non-nuclear principles.

The sensitivity of the nuclear issue has not yet loosened its power. As in other western countries, the number of communities declaring nuclear free zones is increasing in Japan. In 1986 there were 840 such communities in Japan, compared with 180 in Britain, 154 in West Germany and 400 in the Netherlands. In 1987 when the Co-ordinating Committee of Non-Nuclear City Declaration Communities (*Hikaku Toshi Sengen Jijitai Renraku Kyogitai*) held its second annual meeting, they reported that as of March 1987 this number had risen to 1067, including seven prefectures and 400 cities.[34]

The Japanese government will probably continue to support the three non-nuclear principles. Public opinion polls, however, while invariably showing a majority against Japan's developing its own nuclear capability, indicate public awareness of the alleged erosion of the third principle of not introducing nuclear weapons into Japan. In a September 1981 poll 37.4 per cent supported the transit of American nuclear weapons through Japanese territorial waters and airspace; 43.1 per cent however opposed. This result was confirmed three years later when 34.3 per cent favoured transit and 3.2 per cent were in favour of abolishing the third principle.[35] Even some of the opposition parties are reconsidering their attitude. There appears, however, a strong element of public opinion which prefers to maintain the three non-nuclear principles as a means of limiting the expansion of military force. Many believe that weakening or abandoning the three non-nuclear principles would be a further step towards the eventual elimination of other limitations and restraints on the armed forces.[36]

Elimination of any of the three non-nuclear principles would also cause regional anxieties and give the Soviet Union the opportunity to criticize Japan's defence policy. The alleged erosion of the third principle has already been used by the Soviet Union in the INF negotiation as a justification for the concept, since abandoned, of retaining 100 warheads for its SS-20 deployed in East Asia. The abandonment of the three non-nuclear principles would also seriously erode the credibility of the government's longstanding claim to have no ambition to become a big military power.

Will Japan seek a nuclear capability?

With attention in Japan principally focused on the third of the non-nuclear principles, discussion of the first two has receded into the background in recent years. Non-nuclear principles notwithstanding, however, the government has since 1955 stated on several occasions that the Constitution does not rule out the possession of nuclear weapons for defensive purposes. Having, in its statements, linked the scope of the term 'defence' to the international situation and the progress of technology, the goverment has thus kept its options open. Mr Nakasone took a particularly strong stance on nuclear armament during his brief period as director general of the DA in the early 1970s. In Japan's first defence white paper he explicitly stated that constitutionally

Japan could possess nuclear weapons. This assertion caused a storm of protest in the Diet. The same approach to the interpretation of the Constitution has also been used to establish that Japan is legally entitled to possess biological and chemical weapons. However, the government would also have to change the Atomic Energy Basic Act, leave the NPT (see next chapter), renounce membership of the International Atomic Energy Agency (IAEA) and have the Diet revoke its relevant resolutions before it would be able to initiate a nuclear weapons programme.

Objections to Japan's adherence to the Nuclear Non-Proliferation Treaty have been raised by those who felt that Japan should have the option of the issue of nuclear armament in case the American nuclear guarantee was revoked or in order to pursue a more independent security policy. At the time when the NPT was debated, critics voiced particular concerns about the growing Chinese nuclear arsenal, the Indian nuclear test explosion in 1974 and the weakened role of the US in Asia after the debâcle in Vietnam in 1975. The retention of a nuclear option was publicly espoused by then Minister of Science and Technology Moriyama Kinji, who had to be replaced before the negotiations with the IAEA could go on.[37] There is also in some quarters a growing resentment that France and the United Kingdom are still considered to retain some element of great power status by virtue of their nuclear deterrent, a status not warranted by their economic performance.

Japan today has at least the technical capability to build what has been called a 'bomb in the basement'. However, as long ago as 1975, Imai Ryukichi, a nuclear scientist himself, convincingly argued that despite its technological capacity the nuclear arming of Japan is not possible.[38] Even the development of a token Japanese nuclear capability would risk calling into question the US nuclear guarantee, upon which Japan's defence policy is firmly based. It is just conceivable that a major upheaval in the strategic situation in

Asia, accompanied by a loss of faith in the American security guarantee, could lead to a review of Japanese policy in this respect. However, it would be unrealistic to imagine that any Japanese nuclear capability could replace the loss of the American nuclear deterrent. In addition, any such development would provoke tremendous regional criticism against Japan, and in the end could more than offset the possible gains in having a national nuclear capability.[39]

CHAPTER III

Japan and Nuclear Non-Proliferation

The issue of nuclear non-proliferation provides a link between Japan's national arms control and disarmament measures and the country's multilateral arms control and disarmament policy. When the three non-nuclear principles were announced in 1967 they were added to a policy of the peaceful use of nuclear energy. The Atomic Energy Basic Act of December 1955 provides that research, development and utilization of nuclear energy in Japan are carried out only for peaceful purposes. In contrast with its attitude to unilateral Japanese measures which conflict with the Japanese-American security treaty system, the US is ever more keen for Japan to maintain a strict nuclear non-proliferation policy which sometimes clashes with the country's economic interests in the peaceful use of nuclear energy. This chapter therefore looks at the relationship between Japan's economic and technological interests on the one hand and nuclear non-proliferation concerns on the other in order to evaluate the repercussions on the regional and global nuclear non-proliferation regime.

The 1968 NPT

The 1968 NPT brought the superpower-dominated issue of arms control and disarmament to the attention of the Japanese public. The NPT did not appeal to Japan's peace movement since they did not consider it a means of achieving complete disarmament.[1] More importantly, however, although the public and political discussion in Japan was fuelled by the treaty's security aspects, the American nuclear guarantee and particularly the treaty's inherent discrimination towards non-nuclear states, the prolonged debate focused on economic and technological issues. It was this last consideration which led to the treaty receiving so much attention in Japan.

The Japanese recognized very early the importance of nuclear energy for a country poor in natural energy resources and overly dependent on oil. As a result, the American crusade for 'Atoms for Peace' in the 1950s was welcomed in Japan, where it provided an important technological stimulus for the beginning of an age of nuclear power. In 1955 the American Congressman Cole even discussed with President Eisenhower his proposal to present a nuclear power-plant to the Japanese people to be located in Hiroshima in order to symbolize US dedication to the peaceful uses of nuclear energy.[2] However, by 1967 when the government first commented officially on the NPT, Japan still had only a single 166 megawatt commercial nuclear power-plant. In the ensuing debate Japan's prime interest, like that of other western countries such as West Germany, was that the NPT should not inhibit the peaceful use of nuclear energy and the expansion of the nuclear industry. An associated stumbling block, which delayed Japan's ratification of the treaty for six years after signature in 1970, was its insistence that the safeguard agreement with the International Atomic Energy Agency should neither hurt Japan's commercial interests nor place it in a less favourable position than the European Community countries. Rather than continue the practice of direct IAEA supervision of Japanese nuclear facilities, Japan proposed the establishment of national systems for nuclear material accounting which would enable the IAEA to work through these systems and verify their records and accounts.[3] After negotiations, and following Japanese ratification of the NPT in 1976, a Safeguards Agreement which satisfied the NPT provision was concluded with the IAEA in March 1977. Under this the Science and Technology Agency is responsible for the implementation of safeguards in Japan. Inspectors of its Safeguards Division carry out inspection activities by themselves or in the presence of IAEA inspectors.

The peaceful use of nuclear energy

In 1988 there were thirty-six commercial nuclear power-plants operating in Japan. This capacity of 28,046 MW makes Japan the fourth largest nuclear electricity-generating country in the world (about 10 per cent of total western world capacity), following the US, France and the Soviet Union.[4] Nuclear power now supplies some 30 per cent of Japan's total energy generation, exceeding oil-fired thermal generation (23 per cent).[5] According to government plans, electricity generated by nuclear power is expected to reach a total of 46, 630 MW by 1997.[6] While government research and development spending for research into alternative energies is going down, nuclear energy research funding, like aerospace and advanced technologies funding, is increasing.

Japan is now undertaking commercialization of its entire domestic nuclear fuel cycle (except UF6 procurement, yellow cake and conversion), having begun with the fuel fabrication process. The electric power companies established the Japan Nuclear Fuel Service Co. and the Japan Nuclear Fuel Industries Co. which are planning to construct three key nuclear fuel cycle facilities. The former will start to provide reprocessing services around 1995 and the latter will commence enrichment services by around 1991.[7] The reprocessing plant in Rokkosho in northern Japan is to process 800 tonnes per year. Since reprocessing technology was abandoned by the US, Japan gets some of its reprocessing technology and some reprocessing equipment from France, the United Kingdom and Germany. In reprocessing, France is Japan's most important partner. Up to the present about 10 per cent of Japan's spent fuel has been recycled in Japan, the rest in France and Britain.

Since March 1982 Japan has had an operating pilot enrichment plant (at Ningyo), and a prototype plant began operation in 1987 at about 100,000 SWU (Separative Work Unity)/year. The construction of a commercial gas-centrifuge enrichment plant was licensed in August 1988 and construction started in the same month, with an initial capacity of 150,000 SWU/year from around 1991, to be increased over ten years to 1,500,000 SWU/year. In order to reduce enrichment costs, the Japanese are developing a centrifuge which utilizes carbon fibre reinforced plastics (CFRP).[8]

Also relevant for nuclear non-proliferation concerns is the development of advanced nuclear reactors which involve the consumption of plutonium. In 1982 the Atomic Energy Commission decided on the construction of an Advanced Thermal Reactor (ATR) with a capacity of 600 MWe. This reactor type is supposed to allow the efficient use of plutonium as well as depleted uranium. A prototype of this ATR, Fugen (139 MWe), started operation in 1979.[9]

Japan has also proceded with the development of the Fast Breeder Reactor (FBR) although its proposed completion dates have regularly had to be revised. Following an experimental FBR, Joyo, the construction of the protype FBR,

Monju (270 MWe), was started in 1985. The first commercial FBR is scheduled to start operating in the first half of the 2010s; more cautious estimates suggest that it could be one or two decades later.[10] At present the utilization of plutonium gained by reprocessing spent light water reactor is primarily based on its recycling in light water reactors, the Advanced Thermal Reactor Fugen and the Fast Breeder Reactor Joyo. Ultimately, Japan aspires to the practical use of fast breeder reactors which are considered the most efficient plutonium users.[11]

Japanese-American differences on nuclear non-proliferation

Japan's desire to establish a complete nuclear fuel cycle has caused conflict in the Japanese-American relationship. There is a clash between Japan's desire to have full and uninhibited access to the most advanced nuclear technology and to build up an autonomous fuel cycle for commercial purposes and American concerns about nuclear proliferation by the proliferation of advanced nuclear reactors like the FBR and increased use of plutonium. Since Japan is highly dependent on its American ally as supplier of essential nuclear energy materials and services – enriched nuclear fuel is still about 70 per cent imported from the US, the rest from EURODIF in France – the latter has been using its position in order to make Japan comply as closely as possible with its own non-proliferation policies.

Although reprocessing of spent nuclear fuel, which also generates plutonium, by Japan was commercially feasible in 1975, it had to be postponed for many years because of protracted negotiations between Japan and the US. Under a bilateral agreement of June 1968, the US had the right to veto the reprocessing by Japan or any third country of US-supplied or US-enriched nuclear fuel. At Tokyo's insistence an agreement was reached in September 1977 which allowed the reprocessing of 99 tonnes of spent fuel over the two-year period ending in August 1979. At present, Japan is capable of reprocessing about 210 t of spent fuel per year whereas the nuclear power-plants in Japan produced around 800 t in 1988. The 1978 US Non-Proliferation Act, however, required the administration to strengthen all relevant bilateral nuclear agreements. In 1982 then Prime Minister Suzuki and President Reagan agreed to revise the Agreement for Co-operation in the Peaceful Uses of Nuclear Energy. In order to put the retransfer of plutonium from recycled spent fuel on a reliable basis, Japan sought to get a generic approval for this retransfer. In the absence of a revised agreement, the limitation in time and quantity was extended several times until the new Agreement for Co-operation in the Peaceful Uses of Nuclear Energy valid for thirty years was initialled in January 1987, was signed in November of the same year and entered into force in 1988. In the agreement, the US waived the prior US consensus obligation, adopting a blanket system of 'programmatic approval' of nuclear activities, to replace the current 'case by case approval' method requiring US consent for each case of spent fuel reprocessing or plutonium transportation.[12] The US can revoke this programmatic approval in case of a Japanese violation of the agreement. One of the Japanese obligations under the new bilateral agreement which attracted some publicity is to transport recovered plutonium from the French and British reprocessing facilities to Japan only by aircraft rather than, as hitherto, by ship, in order to reduce the possibility of such material falling into the wrong hands. However, this mode of transportation was still criticized by some as being very risky in terms of hijacking and crashes.[13] As a result of these considerations in the Senate and the intervention by the US Department of Defense and the US National Regulatory Commission (NRC), the passage of the agreement through the Senate was delayed until it finally entered into force in 1988 with the transport mode still being debated. In addition, there seemed to be some 'turf battles' occurring between US agencies; the NRC was unhappy about not being sufficiently consulted by the Department of Energy and the Department of State which were mainly responsible for the negotiation of the agreement.[14] The NRC did not consider the safeguard measures for Japanese plutonium facilities to be sufficient. It also criticized, as being in US national interest, an American guarantee that Japanese exports of nuclear-related equipment to the US would be used only for peaceful purposes and the provision that, in the event of non-compliance, Japan could invoke sanctions against the US.[15] Although this new agreement is much more lenient towards Japan, the Japanese involved in nuclear matters still have rather mixed feelings about the negotiating process. There is some resentment in Japan about American determination to coerce its ally into conforming with its concept of non-proliferation and keep control over Japanese nuclear activities. The Japanese particularly resent such treatment, which casts doubt on their peaceful intentions, from the only country in the world which has used nuclear weapons in war.

Japan's contribution to the NPT regime

Economic self-interest and American concerns about the possibility of nuclear proliferation have motivated Japan to make some valuable contributions to the cause of nuclear non-proliferation. Japan is a constructive and co-operative member of the IAEA and the expanded Japanese nuclear programme has led to a steady annual increase in activities. Japan participates in the London Suppliers Group, which tries to control the export of nuclear-related equipment, and it took part in the International Nuclear Fuel Cycle Evaluation (INFCE), which lasted for two years, as well as in related follow–up working groups. Scientists in Japan are also involved in helping to prevent the conversion of fissionable material for military purposes.[16] Japan contributed actively to the recently concluded treaty on information of nuclear disasters. It proposed to include an information obligation in the event of disaster not only in a civilian nuclear plant but also in military nuclear facilities and nuclear test accidents.[17]

Today Japan is an ardent supporter of the NPT, consistently calling for the strengthening of the NPT regime and appealing to the nuclear weapon states to live up to their treaty obligations by reducing their nuclear arsenals, a subject of widespread dissatisfaction among the non–nuclear signatories. By continuing to press for nuclear disarmament, Japan helps to preserve a climate which allows the NPT to continue. At the same time, the example given by Japan's progress in nuclear technology serves to defuse general concern that NPT provisions tend to constrain and impede the widespread use of nuclear energy. However, the continued dissipation of these concerns depends on how tightly the US pursues its non-proliferation policy.

Japan has played an important role in bringing a reluctant China to a broad acceptance of the nuclear non-proliferation regime. As in so much of its policy, Japan's motivation was economic self-interest. In the early 1980s, Japan wanted to sell civilian nuclear power-plant equipment to a China keen to obtain Japanese equipment and technology. The US was, however, reluctant to allow the export of equipment produced in Japan under American licence. After lengthy pressure Japan finally managed to pursuade China to accept the principles of confining international nuclear proliferation to peaceful ends through agreed IAEA safeguards and to adhere to the associated international agreements. China joined the IAEA in January 1984 and, on 16 March of the same year, Japan and China signed a memorandum on the sale of a Japanese pressure vessel for China's planned Qinshan civilian nuclear power-plant.[18] China has not, however, yet signed the NPT.

A further Japanese-Chinese nuclear agreement was signed in July 1985 after some difficulties over Chinese acceptance of Japanese stipulations regarding measures to be taken in the event of non-compliance with non-proliferation constraints. In the end China accepted IAEA safeguards to ensure that transferred nuclear material and equipment would not be used for any military purpose.[19] Other Chinese nuclear co-operation agreements, with Brazil and Argentina, also embodied IAEA safeguards; at the same time China voluntarily placed some of its civilian nuclear installations under the IAEA control regime.[20] After four years of negotiations a US-China agreement for peaceful nuclear co-operation was finally concluded, which, in addition to safeguards, also provided for American on-site visits.[21] Although China has had its own reasons for submitting to international nuclear proliferation control regimes, Japan played a constructive role in these developments through its insistence on Chinese adherence to internationally agreed practices as prerequisite for any technological and commercial deals. This paved the way for China to attain its most coveted prize: nuclear co-operation with the US.

Until very recently, Japan's nuclear engineering industry was less developed than its counterparts in the US, West Germany, the United Kingdom and France. In 1974 the first nuclear power-station was manufactured in Japan and since then the overwhelming part of these plants has been made in Japan. At the moment the industry is working at half its capacity of six reactors per year. For this reason Japan is interested in exports of nuclear power-plants. However, world market demand has been declining in recent years and it is not easy for a latecomer to enter. Moreover, in some cases Japanese manufacturers of nuclear power-generating or related equipment are still dependent on American licences which may constrain sales to third countries. In

order to get on to the export market Japan has concluded
bilateral co-operation agreements with neighbouring countries.[22] It is co-operating closely with South Korea in the
nuclear field, and a nuclear agreement has been concluded
with China. As in the case of COCOM regulations,
breaches in the non-proliferation regime can always occur.
In March 1980 it was disclosed that the purchase, through a
small company, of equipment for the reprocessing of
uranium by Pakistan was prevented only at the last
minute.[23]

From this survey one can, however, conclude that Japan
has been a responsible user of nuclear energy in terms of
impact on the regional and global non-proliferation regime.
In comparison with exports by French, German and British
nuclear energy-related industries Japan has been so far a neg-
ligible factor. Although Japan may become a more active
exporter of nuclear energy equipment in the future on the
basis of its technological strength, it is safe to assume that
the country will be careful about the implications for its security. This concerns notably China, a military nuclear
power with a growing military potential at Japan's
doorstep. An indication of Japan's concern about this growing power is its attitude concerning the application of
COCOM regulations where, in the case of dual-purpose
items, it takes a more stringent approach than the US.

Informal agreement on the control of missile technology

Arms embargoes and controls on the arms trade have often
been proposed in order to prevent conflicts or to contain
them. The results have not so far been encouraging but the
US continues to promote this approach. Control of the
arms trade offers technologically advanced countries such
as Japan the opportunity to play a constructive role in arms

control and disarmament.[24] One fruit of this approach is Japan's participation in a rare agreement on the control of international arms transfers that bans the export of certain kinds of missiles, their components and their technology to countries which are not parties to the arrangement. While not directly connected with nuclear non-proliferation it is very relevant to nuclear weapon delivery capabilities. At the initiative of the US, the seven economic summit nations (US, Canada, the United Kingdom, France, West Germany, Italy and Japan) worked in secrecy in Paris on this arrangement which, after more than four years, was finally concluded on 7 April 1987 through an exchange of *notes verbales*. It is not a formal agreement, but rather a commitment by each participating member to act in accordance with agreed guidelines when considering the transfer of specific types of missile equipment and technology. Each government will implement these guidelines in accordance with its national legislation. As an agreement it resembles the London Nuclear Suppliers Club or COCOM, although there is no permanent secretariat.

The purpose of the guidelines is to limit the risks of nuclear proliferation by controlling transfers which could contribute toward nuclear weapons delivery systems other than manned aircraft. It can therefore be seen as a further US effort to strengthen the nuclear non-proliferation regime. American concern has been prompted by the spread of missile technology among those developing countries which also have an advanced nuclear programme. The nations of major concern are Iraq, India, Brazil, Argentina, Israel, South Korea, Taiwan, South Africa and Pakistan.[25] All these countries are involved in missile programmes based on technology obtained from major powers, including the US. In 1988 it was the Argentine missile Condor-2 backed by Egypt and Iraq which was declared as particularly worrying.[26] India and Israel are believed to possess nuclear weapons and Pakistan is thought to be very close. South

Africa, Brazil and Argentina are also believed to have extensive programmes to develop nuclear weapons.[27] Even where no nuclear weapon connection exists, the knowledge of ballistic missile technology with the potential for strategic use is a matter of increasing concern. The sale of intermediate range ballistic missiles by China to Saudi Arabia has heightened anxieties about the spread of missiles in the Third World and their potential effect on stability.

The guidelines divide all relevant technology and equipment into two categories: Category I comprising the most sensitive items, which will be effectively barred from sale, and Category II, made up of less sensitive items, sales of which may be permitted on a case-by-case basis after assurances that they will be used only for peaceful purposes. The guidelines do not limit co-operation on manned aircraft or on missiles with a range of less than 300 km or a payload of less than 500 kg. The 300 km range criterion reflects both an assumed theoretical minimum range for strategic missile engagement and practical considerations of achievable constraints, given the existing trade in shorter range missiles. The 500 kg payload parameter is based on an assessment that lack of sophisticated nuclear warhead technology will, for the foreseeable future, preclude the development of smaller or lighter warheads by those states whose nuclear weapon potential is of greatest concern.[28]

In evolving and presenting the arrangement the participants thought it important that the outcome should not be seen as an effort by the seven economic summit countries directed against the Third World, although such perceptions were to some extent inevitable because of the nature of the undertaking and the concerns which had prompted it.[29] Another concern was to involve other nations; the agreement therefore contains a clause which says that 'the adherence of all states to these guidelines in the interest of international peace and security would be welcome'. Both the US and Japan approached the Soviet Union and China (the source of many of the technologies used to improve Brazilian missiles) in what seems to have been a concerted effort by all participants to gain support for the understanding.[30] The reaction of these two powers to these *démarches* appears to have been negative.

One major problem was the concern of all participating countries that the guidelines should have a negative effect on exports of high technology goods. Although many of the items listed are on the COCOM lists anyway, Category II contains a broad range of items such as structural elements or inertial equipment where a distinction between civilian and military use may be difficult. The participants therefore also agreed that the guidelines should not impede programmes or co-operation that could not contribute to nuclear weapons delivery systems such as the provision of launch services or co-ordinated bilateral and multilateral research programmes.[31] In addition, at Japanese insistence, the very stringent list of Category II items initially proposed by the US was reduced and clarified. Clarification was sought not only by being very detailed on the specifications of a given item, but also by introducing the clause 'specially designed for use in the systems in ...', etc. One particular item is carbon graphite in Item 8 of Category II of which Japan is the biggest exporter among the seven participant nations, exporting it to South Korea and Taiwan for the production of golf clubs and tennis rackets.

For the Japanese side, specificity about these items was particularly important not only because they were concerned not to be found to have inadvertently breached the arrangement as a result of loose definitions, but also because, in connection with the ban on arms exports, the government had told the Diet that dual-purpose technology could be exported since it was not possible to make a clear distinction between military use and civilian use items and technologies. It was therefore important (though difficult) to achieve maximum consistency between this stance and the constraints involved in the agreement. European participants showed substantially less concern about these issues.[32]

In the context of this book it is interesting to note that there were two press leaks on the negotiation of the guidelines, both of which occurred in the Japanese economic newspaper *Nihon Keizai Shimbun* and clearly demonstrate Japan's commercial concerns.[33] The first leak occurred at the very beginning of the negotiations in December 1983, highlighting the direction against developing countries and the possible participation of the Soviet Union in the future. It mentioned that the concerned ministries and other government agencies in Japan had started to consult about the possible effect of such an agreement on Japan's industry. To the great relief of American administration officials who feared problems for smooth negotiations the two reports were not picked up in other Japanese newspapers nor by western media.[34]

In Japan, the Ministry of Foreign Affairs and MITI were involved in the negotiations; the Defence Agency, however, was not. Unlike most of the other participants, Japan neither exports missile systems nor, at least for the present, produces any with ranges greater than 150 km. Japan's inclusion is, therefore, further confirmation that no significant agreement intended to regulate or constrain international arms transfers can be concluded without Japan because of its technological base. The same consideration underlies Japan's participation in COCOM, the bilateral 'gentlemen's agreement' between the US and Japan on supercomputers, an informal agreement on the export of chemical agents among major advanced industrialized countries and the London Nuclear Suppliers Group. Without the 1987 arrangement, given the technologies available in Japan's space and missile industries, it would be easy for a foreign country to purchase in Japan components to produce missiles which are not even manufactured in Japan itself. In view of the problems with the effective implementation of COCOM rules, only the future will show how useful this agreement can be.

Nuclear arms control and disarmament in the UN framework

Public anti-nuclear sentiment and the constraints of the Japanese-American security treaty also affect Japan's nuclear arms control and disarmament policies within the UN framework. While the former dictates Japanese support for multilateral arms control efforts, the latter limits the extent to which Japan can underpin that political support with practical technological contributions.

Relevant treaties which Japan has signed so far are (in brackets the year of Japan's adhesion) the Partial Nuclear Test Ban Treaty (1964), the Antarctic Treaty (1960), the Outer Space Treaty (1967) and the Seabed Arms Control Treaty (1971).

Japan is particularly active in the pursuit of a comprehensive nuclear testban (CTB) which has for many years been under negotiation at the CD in Geneva. The Japanese government has not always been so positive in its support of a ban on nuclear testing. When a Japanese fishing boat, the Fukuryu Maru, was covered by radioactive fall-out from an American hydrogen bomb test in the Pacific on 1 March 1954, causing the death of one crew member, Foreign Minister Okazaki told the Diet on 25 March that it was only natural for Japan to support American nuclear testing.[35] The accident, however, gave birth to the peace movement in Japan which put pressure on the government's arms control and disarmament policy. But it was only after the conclusion of the Partial Test Ban Treaty in 1963 that the government finally demanded a comprehensive test ban treaty.

Today Japan behaves more independently on this issue. The CTB negotiations in the CD are in a deadlock because of US opposition to a comprehensive ban. The US reasons that verification technologies are still insufficiently developed to enforce a CTB, but it is widely assumed that at least one reason why the US cannot subscribe to such a ban is that it would inhibit the development of SDI. Despite American opposition Japan has vigorously tried to keep the CTB on the CD's agenda. The Japanese delegation in Geneva has provided several working papers on the verification issue.[36] In June 1984, then Japanese Foreign Minister Abe Shintaro, as the first Japanese foreign minister to do so after Japan had been a member for fifteen years, addressed the CD to propose a step-by-step approach to the CTB, whereby existing monitoring technology is used and then developed in a multilateral framework. As a result, Japan has been co-operating with other countries to develop an international seismic monitoring system which will allow the monitoring of progressively lower yield nuclear detonations and distinguish earthquake waves from nuclear test waves. For this purpose a multilateral seismic data exchange system has been created and has, since 1984, been operating through the global data network of the World Meteorological Organization. The nature and capability of the system has been progressively developed and enhanced; as of June 1987 eight countries are linked together through bilateral agreements for the conduct of seismic tests.[37] New ground was broken when, for the first time, the disarmament division in the Japanese Ministry of Foreign Affairs was given specific funding, receiving ¥33 million in FY 1986 and ¥46 million in FY 1987 and 1988. As a result of both national activities and these developing multilateral efforts, underground explosions of somewhere around 10–20 kt can reportedly be detected. These international efforts and the improvement of the relations between the superpowers have now led to a more positive attitude by the American administration towards the feasibility of meaningful verification of nuclear tests.

Although working towards this long-term goal of a nuclear test ban, the Japanese government has been at pains to express its understanding of the American continuation of nuclear tests and shares the US perception that a test moratorium, as proposed by the Soviet Union (and unilaterally implemented by it for over a year), would not enhance the security interests of the US or its allies. Japan regards a deep reduction in nuclear arms, a reinforced balance in conventional forces, enhanced and expanded confidence-building measures (CBM) and improved verification capabilities as essential preconditions for the application of a CTB.[38] Japanese government specialists, such as the former ambassador to the CD, Imai Ryukichi, acknowledge that the realization of a CTB will be extremely difficult.[39]

On certain other nuclear disarmament issues the Japanese government is now bringing its voting behaviour in the UN into line with its open espousal of US nuclear deterrence as a key element of Japan's defence. Since December 1981 the government has been voting against UN resolutions calling for the non-use of atomic weapons, a ban on neutron bombs and a ban on the deployment of nuclear weapons.[40] It's position on the 'non-use of nuclear weapons' resolution regularly tabled in the UN has changed. In 1961 Japan voted in favour; from 1962–79 it abstained; since then it has voted against the resolution.[41] Japan's support of nuclear-free zones or zones of peace is very restrained.

In 1975 Japan voted in favour of a UN General Assembly resolution concerning the establishment of a nuclear-free zone in the South Pacific as a reaction to French nuclear weapon tests.[42] However, when the idea of a nuclear-free zone for South-east Asia was discussed between the foreign ministers of the ASEAN nations and representatives of the European Community, US, Canada, Japan, Australia and

New Zealand, Japan sided with the US against it. Even when Japanese support for such zones has been forthcoming, it has, as the government has repeatedly made clear, been subject to explicit conditions that were typically explained in the context of the zone of peace in the Indian Ocean:

> First, that it is approved by a consensus of the States concerned, including the nuclear-weapon States; secondly, that it does not undermine the peace and security of the region or of the world as a whole; thirdly, that it is accompanied by an effective safeguard system, including international inspection and verification; fourthly, that it is consistent with the principles of international law, including the principle of freedom of navigation on the high seas.[43]

CHAPTER IV

INF: Japan's quest for equality of treatment

The most important nuclear arms control issues in which Japan has recently been involved were the INF negotiations. What was at stake was not so much Japan's security – although Japan was within range of 162 SS-20 and ninety-five short-range SS-12 and SS-23 launchers – but Japan's place in the western alliance and the notion of indivisible security in the trilateral world of northern America, western Europe and north-eastern Asia. As in the case of safeguards in the nuclear non-proliferation context, Japan wants to be, and to be seen to be, on an equal footing with the two other parts of the trilateral world. However, equality is not easily applied in the case of INF because of the different geographic locations of Europe and East Asia and the resulting difference in military deployment. On the other hand, the INF negotiations highlighted for the first time the importance of East Asia for arms control negotiations, which have tended to be focused on the superpowers and/or Europe. The negotiations demonstrate how an intricate mix of bipolarity and multipolarity adds to the difficulty of negotiating global arms control regimes which affect regional security.[1]

Although the deployment of SS-20 in the Far East started in 1978 and had reached a total of seventy-five launchers by

1981 and ninety-nine by 1982, the INF issue came rather late
to the forefront of political consciousness in Japan and the
other western-orientated East Asian countries threatened by
them (South Korea, the Philippines).[2] Before 1981 the
Japanese government had left the issue to the US and did not
consider it necessary to protest against any one specific missile category while there were so many others which could
also reach Japan.[3] In contrast to the West European NATO
countries which feel much stronger about supplementing
inadequate conventional forces by nuclear forces and were
concerned that failure to counter the SS-20 through
negotiating it away would tend to decouple them from the
US, the Japanese government considered the existing
American conventional and nuclear presence in Asia sufficient to offset additional Soviet missiles. Moreover, the
Japanese public perceived the SS-20s in Asia as being
directed mainly against China (as well as providing a
strategic reserve force against western Europe) and, because
of their insufficient target capability, did not believe Soviet
assertions that they were aimed at US naval and air assets in
the Asian region. It was seen as logical for the Soviet Union
to play down any concern with China in order not to
endanger prospects for a the rapprochement with China,
and instead to use the SS-20 issue to attack the American
presence in Asia. But above all, the Japanese government
does not consider a limited regional nuclear war in Asia to
be likely and tends therefore to consider the question of nuclear force balance in a global rather than regional context.[4]
The government's initial desire to maintain a low profile on
the SS-20 issue was, of course, much assisted by the absence
of any American demand to counter-deploy ground-based
INF in Japan.[5]

The Japanese government's public posture changed to
support of the American and European stance on INF
because of American pressure as well as because of the growing likelihood of an INF agreement focused solely on the

European theatre and ignoring the Far Eastern-based SS-20s. At the same time, the East-West climate was poisoned because of the events in Poland, the Soviet invasion of Afghanistan in 1979 and the shooting-down of KAL 007. In 1981 the government protested to the Soviet Union about the growing SS-20 deployment in Asia and later, in January 1982, demanded their removal.[6] Increasing governmental concern was motivated in particular by:

1. its basic foreign policy goal of being an equal partner in the western camp
2. the perception that an INF agreement which ignored Japanese concerns would severely harm Prime Minister Nakasone, who laid particular stress on his good relations with other western countries

Japan and the Soviet position on INF in Asia

In 1983 the Soviet government started for the first time to make public statements on the Asian INF factor, partly prompted by Japan's outspoken attitude towards the issue. 1983 was notable for Nakasone's adoption of an unprecedentedly strong public posture on defence. It was the year when, on a visit to Washington, he was quoted as having said that he wanted Japan to become an unsinkable aircraft carrier. The Soviet Union reacted angrily and TASS threatened Japan with nuclear annihilation, writing that 'In the present nuclear age, there can be no unsinkable aircraft carrier, and by deploying [American nuclear weapons Japan would be] a likely target for a response strike' and warning that such a strike 'for such a densely populated, insular country as Japan could spell a national disaster more serious than the one that befell it 37 years ago'.[7] At this time, in the INF context, General Secretary Yuri Andropov mentioned shifting some SS-20s from Europe to Asia, a theme repeated in

April 1983 by Foreign Minister Andrei Gromyko in an appeal to the West European countries to come to an agreement. The Japanese were particularly upset that the Soviets sought to justify such measures by claiming that Japan was crammed with nuclear weapons and that Okinawa was an enormous nuclear weapon store.[8] Against this background, Nakasone backed the INF declaration at the Williamsburg summit in May which said that the 'security of our countries is indivisible and must be approached on a global basis'. This became Japan's basic stand point in respect of both the LRINF and subsequent SRINF negotiations. In both cases Japan sought total and global elimination of the weapon system in question.

Incorporating a solution to Japanese concerns into the INF negotiation posed a very difficult and lengthy process. The Far East was, after all, not the major theatre of the INF negotiations. The Soviet Union tried to present the Far East as a separate issue, and the US and Europe tended, at least at times, to accept a special treatment for that region in order to reach an agreement. A Soviet representative, Falin, expressed in 1986 the difference between the European and Asian features in Soviet security policy as follows: 'the medium-range missiles are in an artificial but nevertheless existing relationship between Europe and Asia. Asian security problems were, are and will be for us different from European security problems.'[9]

But, while trying to present the Far Eastern INF as a separate issue, the Soviet Union clearly viewed its Asian-based SS-20s as providing valuable leverage for use against both the Japanese-American security alliance and, in particular, the US nuclear capability in the Pacific. In 1985 the Soviet Union proposed a bilateral agreement whereby it would pledge not to use nuclear weapons against Japan if Japan would confirm its non-nuclear status.[10] Some preparedness to modify the earlier Soviet position of leaving some launchers in Asia while eliminating all from Europe also began to emerge when Foreign Minister Shevardnadze stated during his visit to Japan in January 1986 that if the US would reduce its nuclear missiles in the Far East, the Soviet Union would be ready to respond by reducing its nuclear missiles there, including the SS-20.[11] This point was reiterated in May 1987 when Gorbachev declared that if the US agreed to abolish its nuclear weapons in Japan, South Korea and the Philippines, and reduce its aircraft carriers, there would be no obstacle in the way of a global INF solution.[12] The Soviet Union even tried to use the verification issue of an INF agreement to win some sort of control over US bases in Japan. Soviet arms control negotiator Victor Karpov declared in a September 1987 interview: 'We moreover think that additional inspection and verification is also necessary in those countries, where there are at present no American missiles, but which have American bases, which can be used for transport or storage of missiles, warheads and launchers.'[13]

The INF negotiations were, however, exclusively focused on specific land-based missile systems and US weapons in the Pacific region patently did not fall into this category. The negotiating concept of allowing each side 100 LRINF warheads outside the European theatre raised the unwelcome spectre of US GLCM and/or Pershing weapons redeployed to Alaska and thus threatening the Soviet Far East. Soviet resistance to the worldwide elimination of these weapons therefore gradually evaporated.

Japan's influence on the American negotiation strategy

It was the actual execution of the 1979 double-track position by NATO from November 1983 on which demonstrated to the Soviet Union that its INF stance had failed. Japan's signature under the 1983 Williamsburg declaration helped to bolster the western position and cohesion, although the political costs to Tokyo were incomparably lower than for the European countries which received the American INF systems. An actual Japanese influence on US negotiation strategy can be observed clearly only from 1986; this, as we will see, focused solely on the total elimination of Soviet INF in the Asian theatre.

Faced with Soviet intransigence, the Reagan administration, increasingly keen on an arms control agreement for domestic political reasons, proposed in January 1986 the removal of Soviet and American INF from Europe and a 50 per cent reduction of Soviet INF in East Asia. Following protests in Japan and other Asian countries (mainly China) the US was, however, forced to change the wording from '50 per cent cut' to 'major cut'.[14] This American reversal reflected the growing impact of the Japanese government on the negotiating process. From having been an ally who had reluctantly been brought into the process, Japan had become a partner with a strong voice capable of persuading the US to alter its negotiating stance. In 1986 the American arms control negotiator, General Edward Rowny, visited Japan five times for consultations. Both sides felt the need to institutionalize these talks and the first regular conference on arms control and disarmament took place in Washington in January 1987.

Japan's position *vis-à-vis* the US in the INF debate was strengthened by means of close consultation with China and western Europe. China joined the debate even later than Japan, seeming belatedly to recognize its interest in the elimination of Soviet missiles mainly directed against its territory and the merits of achieving this without the need of offering any Chinese nuclear weapons for destruction in exchange. In the end, however, Japan has been publicly supported by China on its INF stance.

Japan's position on complete removal, however, suffered another setback at the October 1986 Reykjavik Summit where Reagan's proposed 'major cut' of Soviet INF forces in Asia took the form of a reduction over five years of Soviet SS-20 warheads in the Far East to 100, to be balanced by a US entitlement to retain 100 Pershing II warheads in North America. It was not clear where in the US these missiles should be sited; the US mentioned Alaska, which the Soviet union opposed. The American position was also criticized by Henry Kissinger who discounted the deployment of Pershing II even in Alaska as 'irrevelant, if not ridiculous' and foresaw the resistance of America's Asian friends against leaving Soviet 100 warheads in Asia.[15]

The Japanese government was willing to compromise on its stance of complete removal of all SS-20 in Asia only if two conditions were met, one of a diplomatic nature and the other technical. The diplomatic stipulation was that such an agreement would be only temporary, with a firm time-table set for the elimination of the remaining 100 warheads.[16] The technical condition was spelled out by Nakasone himself, who proposed to President Reagan before the Reykjavik summit that the Soviets should be required to concentrate their remaining SS-20 in the Novosibirsk area throughout whatever interim period was negotiated before their eventual elimination.[17] Novosibirsk is about 4700 km from Japan and the accuracy of the SS-20 is believed to fall off dramatically at this range. Japan would thus only theoretically still be within range.[18] In April 1987 Nakasone was reported to have added that Moscow should not deploy the 100 warheads on what could be a maximum of 100 SS-20 missiles, as this would both make verification very difficult and allow an increase in system range. Instead, each missile should have its maximum load of three warheads which would mean the deployment of only thirty-three missiles.[19] This number had also been mentioned in a speech in Canberra by Foreign Minister Shevardnadze.[20] The Japanese government also approached Moscow directly. US Presidential arms control adviser Edward L. Rowny later reported that there were, after Reykjavik, concerted efforts by Japan and China to convince the Soviet Union of the wisdom of total elimination of all INF, including a meeting in the Soviet Union where Japanese and Chinese diplomats argued their case in the presence of Rowny.[21]

In the end it was not so much Japan's influence on the US or the Soviet Union which provided the strongest support for Japan and the other Asians against an agreement at the expense of Asia, but the verification issue. It became clear that it would be immensely difficult to verify the elimination of all the designated INF if each side was permitted to retain 100 warheads and thirty-three associated launchers. The verification problem even over-shadowed the issue of the transferability of the SS-20 from Asia to Europe, which had been at the centre of the public debate in Japan as an argument against a Europe-centred INF agreement. The Soviet Union had never accepted it and instead countered it by pointing to the transferability of the Pershing II from the US to Europe.[22] The verification issue finally led the US to retreat to its initial global stance and to the public position of demanding the dismantling of all INF. The NATO Nuclear Planning Group meeting in Stavanger in May 1987 supported this new American position.[23] The Soviet Union accused the US of backing away from what was agreed at Reykjavik and revived in a strengthened form Shevardnadze's January 1986 proposal that Moscow would agree to remove all its medium-range missiles from Europe and Asia if the US abandoned its nuclear capability in Japan, South Korea and the Philippines and also withdrew its aircraft-carrying fleet beyond agreed limits.[24]

The incorporation of Soviet INF in Asia in the final agreement

On 22 July 1987 Gorbachev announced that he was ready to

agree to a treaty eliminating all medium-and shorter-range INF missiles from Asia as well as from Europe.[25] In an interview with the Indonesian newspaper *Merdeka*, Gorbachev also said that 'The Soviet Union is prepared to assume an obligation not to increase the number of its nuclear capable aircraft in the Asian part of the country, provided the US does not deploy in that region, additionally, nuclear systems capable of reaching the territory of the Soviet Union.[26] He reiterated earlier proposals for CBM and the reduction of naval activities in the Pacific. He added that 'We do not link this initiative in this case with the US nuclear presence in Korea, the Philippines [and the US Indian Ocean base of] Diego Garcia. We would like to hope, though, that it, at least, will not grow.'[27] Gorbachev had thus renounced earlier Soviet demands that the US should withdraw its nuclear weapons from its Asian bases. In an August 1987 interview with a Japanese journalist, a senior member of the Soviet General Staff, General Nikolai Chervov, went into some details about American nuclear potential in Japan. He particularly mentioned the nuclear capable American F-16 in Misawa as constituting an important part of American forces globally surrounding the Soviet Union. Although Gorbachev had earlier mentioned only the American nuclear weapons in South Korea, the Philippines and the Indian Ocean where the US should not increase its nuclear weapons, Misawa and Okinawa should naturally be seen as being in this list.[28] Marshal Sergei Akhromeyev, however, gave a sharper profile to the Soviet position. When asked at a news conference in Moscow on 23 July 1987 why his country was willing to drop its previous demand that US nuclear capable aircraft in Japan be included in the deal, he was quoted as saying 'If the SU displays good will and makes these steps, we expect that Japan will appreciate this and take steps accordingly.'[29] Although the conclusion made showed that, in the last resort, the Soviets did not view the removal of American forces from Japan as a critical element in an INF agreement which they badly wanted, Akhromeyev's statement makes it clear that the Soviet Union can be expected to revive its demand about the withdrawal of American forces when they judge it appropriate.

Evaluation

The INF negotiating process has established Japan as an important partner in western security consultations, and in particular in arms control negotiations involving Asian security. This will have significant long-term effects on Japan's security policy. The most important result for Japan is not in the field of security, however, but in the fact that it has been treated equally with western Europe and that the principle of a wider interpretation of the indivisibility of western security has been established. This concept had previously applied only to the Atlantic Alliance; it has now been extended to include Japan.

In security terms, the agreement, if fully implemented, will rid Japan of a nuclear threat without the surrender of any part of the American nuclear deterrent and without the threat posed by conventional imbalance like that in Europe. Since the agreement was eventually expanded to include shorter-range INF (SRINF) systems, the Soviet Union will also have to eliminate those thirty-seven SS-12 (deployed at Novosysoyevka, around 120 km north of Vladivostok) which threaten the northern part of Honshu and Hokkaido. The principal Asian winner, however, is China against which the SS-20s were mainly directed and which did not have to risk political capital in diplomatic manoeuvring to achieve this result. Overall, the SS-20s are only a minor part of the nuclear arsenal which the Soviet Union can direct against Japan and other Asian countries. Both superpowers deploy substantial numbers of nuclear weapons in East Asia on ships, submarines and bomber aircraft, a considerable number of them being nuclear cruise missiles. Japanese enthusiasm after the signing of the treaty in December 1987 was thus rather subdued. As if to underline the continuing threat, the signing of the INF agreement coincided with the intrusion of a Soviet TU-16 Badger electronic observation aircraft into Japanese airspace over Okinawa. Such intrusions are not infrequent but on this occasion, since the aircraft did not react to Japanese warnings, the Japanese Air Force for the first time used weapons to drive it away.[30] The two events, the INF Treaty signature and the Badger episode, received simultaneous first-page treatment in the Japanese press.

If the Soviet Union has given more away in Asia than the US, it has done so in order to secure a successful agreement for the European region. However, the agreement will be used by the Soviet leadership both to futher their long-term goal of separating America's Asian allies from their military alliance partner and to improve its image in the region, tarnished as a result of its invasion of Afghanistan and support of Vietnamese expansionism. It is also very relevant to Asian security that the INF agreement has prepared the ground for cuts in the strategic forces as a result of the START negotiations. Such an agreement could reduce Japanese confidence in the adequacy of the remaining American deterrent and, if so, raise consequential questions about the need for Japan itself to take greater steps to assure its security. This Japanese perception could be enhanced by American troop withdrawals from East Asia and worsening trade relations between the US and East Asia.

CHAPTER V

Regional stability and arms control

Regional arms control and security of Japan

Despite the recent experience of the INF negotiations, the concept of regional arms control is still not on the agenda of Japanese policy-makers, nor on those of most other Asian countries. So far, no significant regional arms control initiatives have emanated from Asia. There are various reasons for this. First of all, there is no specific regional forum to consider the issue. Secondly, arms control is still considered to be primarily the concern of the superpowers, concentrating on nuclear weapons. Kimura Hiroshi also argues that the 'Europe first, Asia next' perception of the other western countries has delayed arms control in Asia.[1] Thirdly, the notion of arms control as part of a comprehensive regional security policy is only gradually being understood. The idea of constraining an adversary's power by mutual and negotiated limitations and restrictions is still very alien to Japanese and other Asian policy-makers, nor is there any obvious possible enthusiasm for engaging in the laborious process of negoitiating arms control measures. Fourthly, geographic conditions, the diffusion of power and the asymmetrical nature of military force deployment make regional arms control in the Asia-Pacific region even more difficult than in Europe, where its continental features, the clear cleavages between two power blocs and the focus on land-based forces should, at least in theory, make arms control goals clearly identifiable and potentially achievable.

Finally the Japanese don't perceive the strategic situation in the region to be as alarming as do the West Europeans. East Asia appears stable; economic development and even political liberalization seem to be the order of the day. A new Korean conflict continues to be avoided despite frequent warnings from South Korea and the Pentagon. The Sino-Soviet relationship continues to improve. As long as the US maintains sufficient military strength in the region and continues to upgrade its capabilities, Japan's political leaders feel little pressure to think of arms control measures. Although the US constantly presses Japan to do more for both national and regional defence against the Soviet threat, both countries agree that, at least for the present, the threat can be better met by the Japanese-American security treaty system than by arms control. Japan's leaders understand that American pressure on Japan for more defence efforts is motivated less by a Soviet threat getting out of hand – although rhetoric sometimes may suggest the contrary – than by growing US financial difficulties which threaten to curtail the US military presence in the region. Any Japanese regional arms control initiatives would almost inevitably have an impact on US force deployments and thus be highly likely to cause yet another dispute in the Japanese-American relationship and add to the problems of military co-operation between Japan and the US. The taking up of regional arms control initiatives by Japan would blur the Soviet-orientated threat perception and thus hamper the growing popular consensus in Japan on doing more for defence and working more closely with the US. It would encourage those popular sentiments which see the threat to Japan's security coming not so much from the Soviet Union as from

Japan's military alliance with one of the superpowers.

Crisis stability of nuclear deterrence in Asia

The question is, however, whether the status quo rests on a reliable basis which provides the crisis-stability so essential to a
region which has seen many upheavals in the past. The Korean
situation will remain volatile even if domestic calm is finally
established in South Korea by effective democratization.
South Asia and South-East Asia are far from being stable.
China is increasingly becoming an assertive naval power as
some skirmishes in the South China Sea over the sovereignty
of the Paracels and Spratley islands have demonstrated.
Finally, the growing Japanese military potential against the
background of weakening American political and military
influence over Japan may revive fears of Japanese regional
predominance. The most immediate challenge may be the
threat to the economic prosperity of Asia posed by
growing worldwide protectionism. Economic disruptions
may increase the dangers of internal instability in many Asia
countries which may lead them to increase their military
forces.

   It is against this background that the major component of
the current security situation in Asia must be seen. Three
nuclear powers are present in the region, and the strategy of
the two superpowers is heavily dependent upon nuclear
weapons. The important role of the nuclear component of
the American forward maritime strategy is particularly
relevant.[2] There is, moreover, a continuing and seemingly
open-ended arms competition in the conventional as well as
the nuclear field between the two superpowers, which is
also recognized by some Japanese observers.[3] The latest
steps in the nuclear field are the deployment of Tomahawk
cruise missiles on units of the US 7th Fleet and air-launched
cruise missiles on Soviet bombers. Because of their dual

capabilities Tomahawks are extremely difficult to bring into an arms control regime, although major attempts are being made to achieve this in the START negotiations.[4] In November 1986 the Department of Defense announced that US army forces in South Korea would be equipped with Lance battlefield weapons capable of carrying nuclear weapons.[5] The Korean peninsula is clearly an area where renewed hostilities remain a genuine possiblity and where any significant North Korean military success could conceivably trigger a nuclear response. Another risk is that of the region being drawn into superpower conflict as a deliberate act of 'horizontal escalation'. This would, of necessity, be predominantly nuclear in character and, in a recent article, Desmond Ball has argued that a superpower naval conflict embodies serious inherent instabilities which greatly increase the likelihood of a rapid escalation to the nuclear level.[6]

In addition to the increase in nuclear weapons and continuing reliance on them, changing deployment patterns are also worrying. Over recent years the superpowers have increased the number and size of military manoeuvres and, in the case of naval exercises, conduct some in closer proximity to each other's borders than formerly. Then US Navy Secretary John Lehman announced to Congress in 1987 that, as a result of the US Navy practice of operating fleet units close to Soviet shores as part of the new forward maritime strategy, the Soviet Navy had changed its pattern of exercises by confining the operations of its fleet units within range of land-based aircraft.[7] In 1988 American and Australian defence sources reportedly said that Soviet naval activities had diminished in size and frequency whereas the qualitative improvement of the Soviet Pacific Fleet was continued. The US is not willing to accept the Sea of Okhotsk as an exclusive Soviet domain. The continuing dispute between the two superpowers about what constitutes international waters could also give rise to conflict. In 1986 the Soviet Union claimed a 'baseline' boundary of thirty-six nautical miles (nm) offshore within which access by foreign vessels is not permitted. However, the US claims the right for vessels to navigate up to three nm off the contour of international coastlines in accordance with international maritime regulations. In May 1987 the nuclear-powered USS Arkansas entered the disputed zone in East Asia to assert the US position; the Soviet Union protested. [8]

A situation with such considerable conflict potential and where military options rely so much on nuclear weapons cannot be regarded as satisfactorily stable. In addition, nuclear arms control measures cannot sensibly be confined to one region only in an age when regional military balances are so interrrelated. It was from this perspective of the interdependence of regional theatres and with the dual capabilities of many modern weapon systems in mind that Robert O'Neill wrote:

> In the interest of stability greater attention will have to be given to the problems created by weapons and platforms which have both nuclear and conventional capabilities. These problems are very difficult to solve but unless there can be established in the Pacific a capacity to limit a war to conventional weapons in the initial stage, there will not be much point in making great efforts to raise the nuclear threshold in Europe. It would be desirable to try to reach agreement on a series of confidence-building measures as soon as political relations in North-east Asia permit. Given that China is also a nuclear power this goal will probably be more difficult to attain than in Europe. [9]

Proposals for confidence-building measures in Asia

It is against this background that Confidence-Building Measures (CBM) are receiving some attention as a first step towards regional arms control and disarmament in Asia.[10] In its first resolution on CBM in 1978, the United Nations General Assembly, on the initiative of West Germany, recommended that 'all states should consider, on a regional basis, arrangements for specific CBM, taking into account the specific conditions and requirements of each region'.[11] A 1985 study by the UN on the naval arms race also includes CBM with its wide-ranging prescriptions.[12]

The Soviet Union, since the early 1980s, has been the most vocal promoter of CBM in East Asia, hoping to see these advance Soviet interests by defusing territorial issues and promoting economic co-operation. Unlike in the Helsinki CSCE process, through which CBM have been developed in Europe, Soviet pursuit of CBM in East Asia would be unlikely to be bedevilled by the issue of human rights. The initial anti-Chinese context of the Soviet moves and the obvious self-serving character of many of the Soviet-proposed measures may not, however, enhance the appeal of the concept to western orientated countries in the region. Since 1969 the Soviet Union has been proposing a 'Collective Asian Security System' which, under Gorbachev, has now become a call for an Asian Security Conference. While the Brezhnev proposal was aimed at isolating China, Gorbachev's initiative not only includes China, but also tries to project recent improvements in Sino-Soviet relations both as the basis of a new Asian security system and as proof that the Soviets are serious.

It was on the occasion of the 26th Party Congress in 1981 that Brezhnev put forward a proposal for CBM in the context of a 'Collective Asian Security System'. In the same year the Mongolians proposed an agreement on mutual non-aggression and renunciation of the use of force among the Asian Pacific countries. In 1984 Gromyko put forward proposals in a letter to UN General Secretary Perez de Cuellar for naval arms control and CBM; the naval aspect is of particular relevance for a region like East Asia.[13] The concrete measures proposed would, however, not impose any limits on Soviet behaviour and are clearly directed against the US which bases its military power in east Asia mainly on maritime forces. The measures put forward by Gromyko called for:

1. no naval activities in areas of conflict or tension;
2. no extended naval deployments by the great powers far from their own shores;
3. withdrawal of vessels equipped with nuclear weapons from certain areas of the Pacific Ocean;
4. limitation of the number of the principal classes of warships world-wide;
5. limits on anti-submarine forces and weapons;
6. limits on naval bases in foreign territories;
7. 'the possibilities of a regional approach to limiting naval activities and naval armaments should be fully utilized';
8. CBM to avert conflict situations and safeguard sea lines of communications.

In practice the implementation of most of these proposals would amount to abdication by the US of its substantial military presence in Asia and other theatres, and would bring the Soviet Union closer to its goal of excluding its rival from the regions around its borders. The proposals reflect Soviet security concerns such as the need for creation of sanctuaries for the Soviet fleet and fear of superior American anti-submarine technology. In a logical extension, the Soviets also try to counter American attempts to persuade Japan to assume more responsibilities for regional security, in particular the security of sea lanes. The Soviets therefore proposed in a May 1985 press commentary to include the discussion of the security of sea lanes 'which would meet the fundamental interests of Japan'.[14] In his Vladivostok speech of 28 July 1986 Gorbachev reiterated his call for a reduction of naval activities, particularly those of nuclear-armed and ASW forces, as well as for measures to ensure the safety of sea lanes, objectives which, as shown above, also coloured the initial Soviet negotiating stance over Asian-based INF. In his July 1987 interview with the Indonesian newspaper *Merdeka*, he made similar proposals:

> Second, I reiterate our readiness for reducing the activities of the naval fleets of the USSR and the US in the Pacific....We would agree to restrict the areas where naval vessels carrying nuclear weapons move so that they would not be able to approach the coastline of the other side within range of their on-board systems. We would agree to curb the rivalry in antisubmarine warfare systems, ban ASW activities, including air ASW activities, in specific zones. Confidence would be enhanced by limitation of the scale of naval exercises or manoeuvers in the Pacific and the Indian Ocean and in the adjoining seas: no more than 1 to 2 major naval (including naval aviation) exercises or man- oeuvers annually, prior notification of their conduct, mutual renunciation of naval exercises or manoeuvers in international straits and adjoining areas, and of the use of combat weapons in the course of exercises in the areas of traditional navigation. This 'model' could be tested in the northern Pacific where there are few 'actors' and then this practice could be extended to cover the southern part of the Pacific Ocean, other countries of the region.[15]

In his September 1988 speech in Krasnoyarsk Gorbachev went even further and promised that his country would not increase the number of nuclear weapons in the region, suggested multilateral consultations concerning freezing of force operations and force numbers and proposed to give up Cam Ranh Bay if the US would withdraw from its military bases in the Philippines.[16]

Similarly, the Soviet Union tries to weaken American military deployments in Asia by encouraging anti-nuclear sentiments. One approach is to propose a treaty which says that the Soviet Union will not use nuclear weapons against countries which have a non-nuclear status. Another is the support of nuclear weapon-free zones. The Soviet Union supports the New Zealand policy of not permitting visits by nuclear-armed ships and has signed the Protocol of the Treaty of Raratonga established by the South Pacific Forum of August 1985, the signatories of which oppose the stationing of nuclear weapons and the conduct of nuclear tests in the region.

The concept of naval CBM poses inherent difficulties and the problems are compounded by the fact that the navies of the two superpowers are fundamentally so different in importance, purpose and design. There seems to be yet no indication that the Soviet Union recognizes this.[17] Although the 1986 Conference on Disarmament in Europe for the first time included naval CBM, they were regulated only in so far as they related functionally to military activities on land in Europe. The unbalanced and self-serving nature of the Soviet proposals outlined above give them no chance of acceptance; they may indeed have diminished prospects for negotiating CBM. It is too early to make a judgement as to whether there has been a qualitative change of Soviet policy towards Asia under Gorbachev. This could be confirmed only by a change in one fundamental aspect of Soviet policy towards Asia: namely the unequivocal abandonment of the use or threat of force complete with associated changes in force structures and deployment. It is for this lack of any such adjustments that an influential Soviet specialist in Japan, Prof. Kimura Hiroshi, has concluded that Gorbachev's government has not yet come up with an original policy for Asia and the Pacific.[18]

Although the Japanese government welcomes the idea of CBM in principle as long as the specific conditions of each region are taken into account, it is very guarded regarding the application of CBM to East Asia.[19] Official reactions to

Soviet advances has been rather negative. In 1981 the Japanese government rejected the Soviet proposals, saying that the situation in the Far East is different from that in Europe and that the automatic transfer of the European CBM concept to Asia is unrealistic. American opposition to the Soviet proposals also makes a positive Japanese attitude very unlikely.[20] The government fears again, as mentioned before, that the growing consensus for more Japanese defence efforts would be reduced by any official advancement of proposals for CBM in Asia, even for measures which would be more practical and balanced than those put forward by the Soviet Union. So far as the proposal for an Asian security conference is concerned, on 23 May 1985 Foreign Minister Abe Shintaro listed the following conditions:

> 1. The US participates in the forum; 2. the proposal does not mean perpetuating the present occupation of four northern islands east of Hokkaido, seized from Japan after World War II; and 3. disarmament by the US and the Soviet Union progresses and the Kremlin moves toward disarmament in Asia as well. But, if the Soviet proposal is the same in substance as the Asian collective security scheme proposed in 1969...Japan would take a negative stand toward the proposal.[21]

The idea of a regional security conference has been taken up by the Soviet side on several occasions. When Japan's foreign minister Uno proposed to his visiting Soviet counterpart in December 1988 to reduce tension in the region by releasing data about the size of Soviet forces in the region, he was told that this could be done in the context of regional talks on demilitarization.[22]

Nevertheless Japan has an interest in furthering the cause of naval arms control since it depends heavily on the freedom and security of sea lanes for its economy (in 1983 Japan imported 550m. tons of goods via its sea lanes).[23] In addition, Japan may become isolated regionally against the background of improving superpower relations, closer Sino-Soviet ties and an improved Soviet image after the withdrawal from Afghanistan, while its relations with the Soviet Union remain stagnant. In order to evaluate possible Japanese reactions to Soviet arms control proposals it is therefore necessary to look more closely at the main stumbling bloc in their relationship, the territorial conflict.

The territorial conflict

In public statements, the Japanese government takes the line that, if the Soviet Union is really serious about confidence building, it should acknowledge the existence of the territorial dispute and, in the spirit of its purposes, make the first move by withdrawing troops from the disputed islands. Since the Soviet military build-up has an intimidating effect on Japan, a reduction of troops or sophisticated weapon systems would have a beneficial effect. Such a Soviet move appears, however, unlikely. The Soviet Union under Gorbachev seems as unwilling as under previous leaders to compromise on territorial issues. The Japanese government, however, stands by its territorial claim, believing that the Helsinki proccess was made possible only by West German recognition of the territorial status quo in Central Europe. To put it briefly:

> The Soviet Union has no overriding interest in obtaining international recognition of borders in East Asia as she has in Europe. The disputed territories in East Asia (Northern Territories and parts of China) are not 'sovereign' states under its tutelage. But the Soviet Union has also nothing to offer in return as substantial as in Europe: there are no Japanese left on the disputed

Northern Territories, and thus there is no eager American ally like Germany in Europe, which is interested in making compromises in order to secure the human rights of its nationals on the other side and to draw the US and other countries into a Helsinki-type process.[24]

Recent developments have introduced the possibility of some movement on the Northern Territories issue and could, over time, affect Japanese-Soviet relations in general and the issue of CBM in East Asia in particular. As a result of Foreign Minister Shevardnadze's visit to Japan in January 1986, negotiations for a peace treaty were resumed and, according to Japanese understanding, include discussion of the territorial dispute.[25] In 1986 the Soviets allowed the resumption of Japanese grave visits to tend ancestral graves on the islands without passports or visas being required. These visits had been stopped in 1976 when the Japanese government refused a Soviet request for passports. In Japan a debate is taking place about whether the two sides should first try to ameliorate their bilateral relationship and then later discuss the teritorial issue (an approach designated as *deguchi ron* in Japanese) or whether settlement of the territorial issue is a prerequisite for improvement of relations (*iriguchi ron*). The bilateral fishery agreement of 1977 has shown that when vital interests are at stake (and enhancing stability should fit this category) the territorial issues can be finessed. Article 8 of that agreement reads:

No prescription in this agreement shall be taken to violate the position or opinion of either government with respect to...issues in the [two nations'] mutual relations.

In contrast, a 1973 agreement on migratory birds was ratified by the Japanese side only in December 1988 for lack of a similar clause; the political or economic significance of this agreement is, however, minimal. The treaty had mentioned two species of birds on the disputed territories and Japan agreed to its ratification after the Soviets had changed the text.[27]

Specific applications of CBM in North-East Asia

The only agreements concerning East Asia which could be considered as CBM are the 1972 Agreement between the US and the Soviet Union on the Prevention of Incidents at Sea and the conclusion of an agreement in November 1985 on increasing the safety of civilian air traffic in the North Pacific in the aftermath of the shooting-down of the Korean airliner, KAL 007. Japan is a partner to the latter agreement, as a result of which aviation control centres in Tokyo, Anchorage and Khabarovsk will exchange information when civilian airliners encounter problems, and the Tokyo and Anchorage centres will advise Khabarovsk when airliners enter the Soviet flight information region (FLIR).[28] As in the case of the Japanese-Soviet fishing agreement, a clause was introduced which handled the territorial conflict between Japan and the Soviet Union, 'Recognizing that each state has complete and exclusive sovereignty over the airspace above its territory'. With the expansion of the Japanese Navy's number of vessels and missions it may be appropriate for Japan and the Soviet Union to conclude an agreement on the Prevention of Incidents at sea as has been done between the Soviet Union and the United Kingdom and is planned between the Soviet Union and France.

The area most urgently requiring CBM in East Asia is the Korean Peninsula.[29] In 1971, and several times since, the US has proposed that steps be taken genuinely to demilitarize the so-called Demilitarized Zone (DMZ). None of these proposals have received any positive response from North Korea. From 1982 onwards, the US has invited North Korea to send military observers to the annual joint South Korean-American Team Spirit manoeuvre. The North Korean response has been predictably negative; acceptance would have amounted to a legitimization of the American military presence in South Korea. In October 1984 President Reagan stated in his UN General Assembly speech that CBM would be 'an important first step toward peaceful reunification'.[30] The North Korean side expressed interest and proposed trilateral talks between itself, the US and South Korea to include discussions of possible CBM. The American side declined to participate in such talks, and suggested instead that CBM should be considered within the Military Armistice Commission in Panmunjom. When North Korea finally agreed and in 1985 tabled some proposals for tension-reducing measures within the Joint Security Area, the US rejected them as too one-sided. In 1986 North Korea used the Team Spirit manoeuvres as a pretext to withdraw from the North-South dialogue.[31]

The Korean peninsula has always been considered of great concern for Japanese security. The Japanese government has expressed the view that any war in East Asia would be most likely to begin on the Korean peninsula. It would therefore seem natural for Japan to propose CBM for the area but this has not been the case so far. In addition, since Japan has no diplomatic relations with the North, there are few channels of communication with Pyongyang. Japan has, however, contributed to the economic welfare of South Korea and encouraged both sides to resume the North-South dialogue. In consultation with Seoul, Japanese government leaders have raised the Korean situation at summit meetings in order to get an understanding among the other western leaders. On the occasion of the Olympic games in Seoul, Japan was an important actor in ensuring the security of the event and both countries worked closely together to prevent terrorist attacks. When a high ranking Japanese politician suggested in 1988 that Japan might act as a go-between in the growing Korean-Chinese relationship, South Korean reaction was very negative.

There are two principal reasons which limit Japan's capability to become more actively involved in reducing tensions on the peninsula. The first is South Korean sensitivity towards any Japanese political involvement in its affairs because of the tragic history of Japanese-Korean relations, compounded by fierce Korean nationalism. Any such Japanese initiative would have to be put forward with considerable delicacy of tone if the mere fact of its Japanese origin is not to invite rejection by both Korean states. The second is lack of American interest in having Japanese support because of the Administration's conviction that Korean affairs are an American concern, particularly when they concern military matters like CBM.[32]

The US attitude on Japan's involvement has been changing slightly since 1987 because of Japan's growing political power and political intention to speak for East Asia in international forums like the Economic Summit Meeting. In April 1987 the US informed North Korea that it was prepared to take major steps to ease relations between the two countries if the North-South talks were resumed and if Pyongyang agreed to take part in the 1988 Olympic Games in Seoul. It was announced that the US had discussed these steps with South Korea, the Soviet Union, China and Japan.[33] After the North Korean directed bombing of a South Korean airliner in November 1987, killing 115 people, the atmosphere again became less conducive to improved relations. After the successful conclusion of the Seoul Olympics in September 1988 it seems that the initiative for an improvement of North-South relations and CBM has shifted to South Korea.

The low-key attitude of the Japanese government towards arms control and CBM on the Korean peninsula has given the political left the opportunity to stake out an independent line on Japanese-Korean relations by actively promoting such measures and establishing direct links with North Korea. In March 1981, for example, the North Korean Labour Party and the Japanese Socialist Party (JSP) jointly proposed the establishment of a nuclear-free peace zone in North-East Asia. They advocated a test ban, as well as a ban on the development, possession and introduction of nuclear and chemical weapons in North-East Asia.[34] Although the JSP is now willing to acknowledge the legitimacy of the South Korean government and to send party leaders to South Korea, the Seoul government has been reluctant to grant them visas because of what they consider their pro-North Korean stance.[35]

Some Japanese academics, encouraged by the successful continuation of the Helsinki process in Europe, are starting to show interest in CBM proposals for their region. Iwashima Iwao, former professor at the National Institute for Defence Studies in Tokyo, has proposed the concept of a multinational non-governmental organization for the monitoring and prevention of Pacific conflicts. However, his proposal would exclude the two superpowers and thus significantly reduce the likely crisis-management capability of any such arrangement. He also put forward CBM for the Korean Peninsula, noting particularly the American proposals for improved US-North Korean relations.[36] Professor Sakamoto Yoshikazu has proposed the establishment of a UN regional disarmament committee, charged with research, data assembly, public relations, discussions and negotiations.[32] Col. Nakamura Yoshihisa, who studied arms control at Stanford University and has been teaching at the Defence University for over ten years, has written an article in which he emphasizes the positive role of CBM for deterrence. He argues that an exaggerated public evaluation of the Soviet threat promotes the Finlandization of Japan, and that military CBM would reduce this erroneous threat perception. He also proposes specific CBM designed to reduce the risk of an accidental war and a surprise attack.[38]

Another academic, Yamamoto Takehiko, bases his article on arms control in East Asia on the experience in Europe and suggests that Japan should now take the initiative and begin to reduce the size and number of its military manoeuvres. The territorial issue should be set aside for the time being and a Helsinki–like multilateral negotiation process should be started, including the superpowers, at which military CBM should be worked out.[39]

CHAPTER VI

Japan's role in the Geneva Conference on Disarmament

Among the various multilateral arms control forums, the most substantive work is done in the forty-nation Conference on Disarmament (CD) in Geneva. Japan has been member of this group and its predecessors since the early 1970s. Although there are eight other general topics on the agenda of the CD, its priority has always been the issue of nuclear weapons. For this reason the Comprehensive Test Ban (CTB) has always attracted the greatest attention from the Japanese side.

Convention on Chemical Weapons

Next to the CTB issue, Japan has shown interest in the Convention on Chemical Weapons upon which the CD has worked for many years. Japan is a signatory of the 1925 Geneva Protocol on chemical warfare, but has frequently declared that the Constitution does not interdict the use of chemical weapons for self-defence. However, in the case of chemical weapons Japan has no direct security interests at stake since it does not feel threatened by chemical weapons to the same extent as do European countries nor does it consider chemical weapons necessary for protecting the balance of power between the superpowers in East Asia.

Japan's interest in the detail of the proposed convention stems primarily from the fact that a myriad of technical information is put forward to the relevant working group and from the need to shape the convention in such a way as to minimize the extent to which Japan's advanced chemical industry will be affected by restrictions and verifications. This concern about effects on the chemical industry has been mentioned on several occasions by the Japanese CD representative.[1] The Japanese side has thus taken great interest in the third item of the planned convention, dealing with the non-production of chemical agents which can be used for chemical weapons. With the growing likelihood of an agreement the Japanese chemical industry has been showing increasing concern about the effects of the verification measures being negotiated (protection of commercial secrets, intrusiveness of on-site inspections and the possibility that the measures will reveal inadequate safety measures in some small and medium-sized Japanese companies). As a result, a special government effort has been mounted to convince industry of the merits of the planned convention.

Although the convention is the most promising item on the CD agenda, Japan has not been particularly active in providing working papers to advance the negotiations. There was a contribution in July 1985 on 'The application of [nuclear] safeguards remote verification technology to verify the chemical weapons convention' in which Ambassador Imai, based on his personal and intimate knowledge of IAEA safeguards, examines the verification experience gained in the nuclear field and its applicability to a chemical weapon ban.[2] Verification in this case involves remote sensing and associated data transmission telecommunications, areas in which Japan could make a substantial contribution. Japan's direct interest is to have a verification technology which is as unobtrusive as possible. The latest Japanese working paper of 30 July 1987 on the verification of non-production of chemical weapons demonstrates the same concern about verification. It is concerned with clarifying the difference between non-production of chemical weapons *per se* and the monitoring of the production of certain substances in the chemical industry.[3] Given an acceptable verification regime, Japan appears more willing to conclude a ban on chemical weapons than do the US and some West European countries.[4]

While the CD is taking its time to find a consensus for the chemical weapon convention among forty countries, the actual or suspected use of chemical weapons has increased, as events in Indochina, Afghanistan and particularly the Iran-Iraq war have shown. It has become clear that even less developed countries can develop conventional chemical warfare agents from commercially available chemical substances. According to the US Pentagon, the number of nations with programmes in offensive chemical warfare grew between 1972 and 1988 from seven to twenty.[5] When reports and physical proofs of the use of chemical warfare agents increased in 1986, several advanced countries tried to impose relevant export controls. MITI officially contacted the chemical industry and chemical trading companies to urge restraint on the export of forty types of chemicals, including potassium cyanide and hydrogen fluoride.[6] This administrative guidance was part of a concerted effort by several western industrialized countries similar to the in-formal agreement on the export of missile technology and equipment made public in April 1987. The importance of controlling the export of certain equipment and substances was demonstrated in September 1988 when the US ex-pressed concern to Japan that a Japanese company's machine tool delivery to Libya had helped the country with the pro-duction of poison gas.[7]

Prevention of an arms race in outer space

Negotiations on the prevention of an arms race in outer space have become a central item in the CD since the establishment of the Ad Hoc Committee on this topic. Concerned by the research activities of both superpowers into the military use of space, the Japanese delegate made Japan's interest clear by saying 'As my country is making efforts to develop technologies for peaceful uses of outer space, we have a great interest in this subject and we intend to make endeavours so as to contribute to the work of this Conference in this respect'.[8] However, the work of this Committee has not progressed very far because there are basic differences on what would constitute an arms race in outer space and for lack of technical information which can come only from the two superpowers. Meanwhile reconciliation of Japan's position on the issue with its participation in the US SDI programme remains a potential source of embarrassment for the government. When, in February 1987, some senior US Administration officials (Weinberger, Perle) mentioned early deployment of at least part of an anti-ballistic missile system, the Japanese government was greatly embarrassed because it made a Japanese decision on an SDI agreement with the US even more difficult. More important in the long run, however, is that the government could only remind the US of its five principles on SDI which Nakasone had spelled out in January 1986, and which also contain the principle that SDI should not run counter to the ABM Treaty. Apart from this, the government's position is that it has to accept the American interpretation of the Treaty and leave it all to the two signatories.

CHAPTER VII

Japan's technological capabilities and arms control verification

The growing Japanese involvement in actual or putative arms control agreements, such as the CTB, NPT and the planned convention on chemical weapons, raises the general issue of the possibility of Japan contributing to arms control verification on the strength of its technological capabilities and in particular its potential for developing national technical means. As discussed earlier, Japan now possesses the technology to produce communications and surveillance satellites, although their performance is not yet as advanced as those of the superpowers or France.

Third countries may, by virtue of their independence or neutrality, offer more acceptable means of verification for some types of arms control, although the bilateral nature of most arms control agreements is still considered unconducive to third country involvement.[1] Japan might qualify for a role in any such 'independent' verification regimes since, although it is not a neutral country, the thrust of its high technology and space programme is non-military. Such a contribution could provide a welcome additional market for the participating Japanese companies. This commercial interest is beginning to be recognized. An informal group, the *Mitsubishi Soken Teisatsu Kenkyukai* (Mitsubishi Observation Research Group), has been organized to promote the development of advanced remote-sensing satellites for a 3-400 km orbit, which, although primarily considering commercial applications such as discoveries of earth resources, does not exclude providing services for arms control-related purposes. A proposal for a Japanese contribution to arms control verification was made in 1982 by the former rector of the United Nations University in Tokyo, Soedjatmoko, when he proposed that Japan should offer to the UN a communications and surveillance satellite.[2] A similar proposal had been made by Adlai Stevenson in 1981.[3] More recently, Professor Iwashima Iwao has proposed that Japan should contribute to setting up a satellite system for the Korean Peninsula, initially to observe the military movements of both Korean states and later to provide a verification system to underpin any agreed arms control measures for the area.[4] Imai Ryukichi offered, moreover, a very interesting political rationale for Japan becoming involved in arms control verification issues. After having discussed the technical and political aspects of verification of superpower as well as multilateral arms control arrangements, he argues that third country involvement in arms control verification mandatory is essential:

> If such is the reality of the compliance diplomacy today with national security of the superpowers at stake, then what is required of the rest of the world is more than usual determination to cultivate means of active and real involvement and participation in this novel form of diplomacy. The efforts in this direction do not guarantee success, but the price of not exerting efforts is to be left out, and at the worst, become irrelevant to the arms control and disarmament today.[5]

In his article he particularly stresses the problems which may arise in connection with space disarmament. He warns the non-superpowers of the dangers of being invited by the superpowers to be merely interested bystanders or of being put off by them from a multilateral disarmament regime in space because of the problem of non-verifiability. He therefore proposes:

> The only way to avoid either of the two traps and find ways of meaningful participation in a possible multilateral space disarmament regime is to increase technical and other capabilities to understand and appreciate the status of militarization and to be in a position to promote (a) a consistent strategy for peace in outer space as well as useful verification measures. Merely declaratory policies of space disarmament, although effective as instruments of public diplomacy...often create [the] exact reverse of meaningful participation by diverting attention away from technical and military realities into more abstract and thus non-implementable theses.[6]

Prime Minister Nakasone showed particular understanding of the necessity of verification for arms control agreements and realized that Japan, as a major technological power, could contribute to it. On 29 January 1985 he told the Diet that he had offered President Reagan a Japanese contribution to the strengthening of verification through research and other assistance.[7] The idea of a Japanese contribution to verification was repeated the following month by Nakasone and his foreign minister Abe Shintaro in the course of a Diet interpellation where both endorsed the idea in general terms.[8] These two proposals have not been repeated since then. There has been no known reaction from the US, and a US interest in Japanese assistance in verification appears unlikely, at least for the present.

Working against Japan becoming a partner in verification of arms control agreements is superpower reluctance to see other countries developing surveillance capabilities equalling their own. Verification technology is as advanced and its secret as closely guarded as those of weapons themselves.[9] The success of the INF agreement and the new vigour thus given to arms control and disarmament may, however, change attitudes to verification. The INF agreement, which appears simple and easy compared with the problems posed by the implementation of a possible START agreement, has also demonstrated the enormous costs of arms control which may hasten a reorientation of attitudes towards some non-superpower verification contribution. In September 1987, even before the signing of an INF agreement, Mikhail Gorbachev called for the creation of a mechanism under the UN for 'extensive international verification of compliance with accords to lessen international tensions, limit armaments and for monitoring the military situation in conflict areas'. [10] He did not, however, make any detailed proposals nor yet suggest how such a highly expensive regime might be funded. However, the peace-keeping and peace-creating functions of the UN have recently been re-evaluated more positively by many states, notably the Soviet Union, because of some success in helping the superpowers to come to terms in Afghanistan and assisting Third world countries involved in wars to embark on negotiations.

CHAPTER VIII
Conclusions

We have seen that Japan, by virtue of its political, military and economic/technological interests, has become involved to a considerable extent in arms control at a national, regional and global level. Its unilateral disarmament and arms control measures have become diluted because of its security interests, the demands resulting from a military alliance with a nuclear superpower and commercial interests. The major exception to this dilution is the nuclear non-proliferation area where the strong interests of its American ally and Japan's dependence on it have actually resulted in the encouragement and strengthening of the country's nuclear non-proliferation policy. The INF agreement has for the first time involved Japan in a superpower arms control agreement, and it has proven that it could influence the outcome in some way although its immediate interests were much less at stake than was the case with Europe. Interest in regional arms control and CBM is still very low. The inhibiting factors are a basic satisfaction with the security arrangements with the US and the territorial issue *vis-à-vis* the Soviet Union.

The question is whether present Japanese contributions to arms control are sufficient for a power like Japan. We have seen that there are important political, military and economic/technological reasons why Japan should do more. It is clear that Japan cannot protect its various interests in many arms control-related forums like the CD in the future by mere damage limitation policy. Reaction to political concerns by Japan's neighbours and the US may in the end provide the greatest impetus for greater Japanese contribution to arms control. The government stresses in every statement on foreign policy that Japan will never become a 'military power' or 'big military power' (*gunji taikoku*). In relation to Japan's growing military potential it does not seem to be very clear for Japan's neighbours where the Japanese will draw a line. Since quantitative and qualitative restraints have proved to be of a temporary nature, it can only mean that Japan will not use military power in order to advance its national interests. In effect, the Japanese government is referring to a range of limitations on the military, such as the renunciation of acquiring offensive weapons like missiles reaching further than 150 km, aircraft carriers, nuclear weapons, as well as to certain organizational features such as the civilian control of the SDF and the maintenance of only a voluntary armed force. Even the American administration is becoming concerned about too much American pressure on Japan to expand its military, Richard L. Armitage, Assistant Secretary of Defence of the Reagan administration, asked in February 1988, of those demanding more Japanese spending on military forces: 'What would the additional funds be used for? A nuclear capability? Offensive projection forces? Professor Kennedy speaks of Japanese carrier task forces and long-range missiles – is that what Congress wants? Will that enhance stability in East Asia?'[1]

If the present reduction of superpower tensions continues, it will increasingly affect East Asia as well. The Soviet Union's rather unbalanced arms control proposals for East Asia may win more sympathy in the region after its withdrawal from Afghanistan, a settlement of some sort in Indochina, the withdrawal of Soviet troops from Outer Mongolia and the re-establishment of party-to-party relations between the Soviet Union and China. Increased trade frictions between the US and East Asia may benefit the Soviet Union. Budgetary constraints may tilt the balance in the US in favour of substantial troop reductions in East Asia. In this case Japan would have a strong interest in not reacting just by offsetting American withdrawals by more of its own defence efforts, but by taking care that the balance of the military force of both superpowers in the region was maintained through well-tuned arms control and CBM. As Hasegawa Tsuyoshi pointed out, Japan will face a strategic crisis if there are no Japanese policies on regional arms control while the Soviet Union is focusing on such proposals.[2]

Japanese participation in verifying arms control agreements is a very interesting example of a positive contribution. The obstacles remain considerable. Japan is considered too much as part of the West rather than a neutral country. The superpowers do not yet want third party involvement in the verification of their bilateral arms control agreements. The Japanese government as a whole does not yet seem to be seriously considering putting forward specific proposals. The idea should, however, not be written off and could increase in its appeal. Low-level, unobtrusive assistance might be proposed to begin with. It is, for example, conceivable that either superpower may prefer to use a certain Japanese technology for certain verification tasks in order not to reveal its own technological capability to the other side. Should participation in regional verification or space observation become a possibility, Japan will have to be cautious about the reaction of its Asian neighbours which may be both suspicious about its ultimate intention or just concerned about Japan's technological advantage.

Despite these problems and others in different arms control-related areas, the concept of a Japanese role remains one worth pursuing, not only in the interest of national security and economic interests, but also in order to project the image of a country which has wider and more responsible goals for its technological achievement then merely utilizing them for its commercial or military ends. The war-renouncing Article 9 of the Constitution and the regular incantation by Japan's political leaders of Japan's never again becoming a big military power lose their persuasiveness in view of a $41 bn defence budget which makes Japan, at least in terms of defence expenditures, rank third after the Soviet Union and the US. Rising to international responsibilities by contributing more decisively to arms control efforts and CBM appears more appropriate for a power like Japan. These efforts cannot just be left to western Europe and the US if they are to be effective and well integrated into the concept of western security as a whole. The indivisibility of western security for which Japan fought so hard in the INF context demands more Japanese input.

Time is pressing for Japan as well as the other East Asian countries. Particularly in view of the recent political changes in Japan, public opinion can be expected to become less tolerant of continued high defence expenditures while other countries in Europe and the US are decreasing their defence efforts. In Europe the longing for a lower threshold of armament and better relations is so strong that it has almost become an irreversible momentum, in contrast to the *détente* period in the 1970s which was not linked to similar domestic changes in the Soviet Union as is the case today. For this reason the Europeans will have little patience with slow progress of the reduction of tension in other regions of the world and will try to continue on their path, even if its changes may be prejudiced by the continued existence of tension in regions like the Asia Pacific. The course of the INF negotiation is the most obvious example for this attitude: the West Europeans and for a time the US also were ready to eliminate all INF missiles from an area ranging from Europe to the Urals, allowing the Soviet Union to shift these missiles from the European part of the Soviet Union to the area east of the Urals and to the Soviet Far East. Only the technicalities of the INF agreement, that is, the impossibility of having a meaningful agreement on missiles which could easily be transferred back to Europe as well as the difficulty of monitoring and verifying such an incomplete and partial agreement, prompted the US to dig its heels in and demand a zero–zero solution. It was therefore not so much the protests of the Japanese government and other Asian governments which insisted on the indivisibility of Western government. The countries of the Asia Pacific region cannot base their peace on the technicalities of arms control agreements (which can be ignored) as the time lag created between the present unstable situation and the start of an irreversible momentum towards the reduction of tensions and arms control may prove too great. The countries of this region cannot leave to others the political, military and intellectual burden of supporting Western and global security through the quest for a fine balance of military preparedness and arms control. They will have to join global efforts to attain this, and Japan will have to play a prominent role in it.

Notes

Introduction

1. Hedley Bull, *The Control of the Arms Race*, London: Weiden-feld & Nicolson (1961), p. ix, and Barry Buzan, *An Introduction to strategic Studies, Military Technology and International Relations*, London: Macmillan in association with IISS (1987), p. 252.

2. For an earlier analysis of these issues by the author, see J.W.M. Chapman, R. Drifte and I.T.M. Gow, *Japan's Quest for Comprehensive Security: Defence-Diplomacy-Dependence*, London: Frances Pinter (1983), pp. 119–39; published in Japan as *Anzen hosho no atarata na bishion*, Tokyo: Ushio (1984).

Chapter I

1. 'Japan's contribution to military stability in north-east Asia', prepared for the Subcommittee on East Asian and Pacific Affairs of the Committee on Foreign Relations, United States Senate, by the US Arms Control and Disarmament Agency, Washington, June 1980.

2. See Reinhard Drifte, 'Disarmament and arms control in

comprehensive national security (CNS)', in J.W.M. Chapman, R. Drifte and I.T.M. Gow, *Japan's Quest for Comprehensive Security: Defence-Diplomacy-Dependence*, London: Frances Pinter (1983), pp. 120ff.

3.   *Asahi Shimbun* (evening edition), 10 June 1982.

4.   Imai Ryukichi, 17 April 1984, Committee on Disarmament, CD/PV, 259, p.15.

5.   Imai Ryukichi, 'Science, technology and diplomacy: a case study on Japan', working paper for the 4 March 1987 meeting of the Study Group on Technological Change and Foreign Policy, Council on Foreign Relations, New York.

6.   Robert O'Neill, 'The balance of naval power in the Pacific: implications for force structure', special exposition supplement ENSA/NAVTEC '86, *Pacific Defence Reporter 1986*, p. 2.

7.   Kuranari Tadashi, 'Japan–US relationship: to further strengthen the partnership between the two countries', Ministry of Foreign Affairs, Tokyo, 19 April 1987.

8.   Nakamura Yoshihisa, '*Shinrai josei sotchi to Nihon no yokuseiryoku* (CBM and Japan's deterrence capability)', *Kokubo*, October 1986, pp. 8–24; Nakamura Yoshihisa, '*Shinrai josei sotchi to boei seisaku*', *Gaiko Jiho*, 1232 (February 1986), 2–15; Nakamura Yoshihisa (ed.) *Shinsedai No Senryaku Shiso* (*Strategic Thinking in the New Era*), Tokyo (1987), pp. 153–74.

9.   Reinhard Drifte, in Chapman, Drifte and Gow, op. cit., p. 134.

10. Interview with a high official of the Ministry of Foreign Affairs, 29 August 1986.

Chapter II

1.   Reinhard Drifte, in J.W. M. Chapman, R. Drifte and I.T.M. Gow, *Japan's Quest for Comprehensive Security: Defence-Diplomacy-Dependence*, London, Frances Pinter (1983), p. 123.

2.   'World military expenditures and arms transfers 1986', Arms Control and Disarmament Agency (ACDA), Washington

(1987), p. 122.

3. *New York Times*, 25 November 1986.
4. *International Herald Tribune*, 13 April 1987.
5. *Korea Herald*, 8–9 June 1987.
6. Reinhard Drifte, *Arms Production in Japan*, Boulder, Colo.: Westview Press (1986), p. 76.
7. Ibid., pp. 78–9.
8. *Journal of Japanese Trade & Industry*, 3 (1987), 7; *Far Eastern Economic Review*, 27 August 1987.
9. *Defence of Japan 1985*, Tokyo: Defence Agency (1985), p. 276.
10. Ibid.
11. *Daily Yomiuri*, 4 January 1984; *Asahi Evening News*, 17 April 1984.
12. *Daily Yomiuri*, 22 February 1985.
13. *Jane's Defence Weekly*, 2 November 1985; *Kyodo* in English, 10 September 1985.
14. *Nihon Keizai Shimbun*, 23 March 1986, p. 1.
15. *Far Eastern Economic Review*, 25 September 1986, p. 29.
16. *Nihon Keizai Shimbun*, 26 July 1987.
17. *International Herald Tribune*, 5 November 1987.
18. *Asahi Shimbun* (evening edition), 8 April 1987 and 10 April 1987.
19. *Kyodo* in English, 6 February 1987; FBIS-APA-97-025, 6 February 1987, vol, 4, no. 025, Daily Report Asia & Pacific. An official of the Ministry of Foreign Affairs involved in the space station negotiations denied this report when asked about this declaration by the author in November 1987.
20. Interview with Dr Richard W. Getzinger, Councillor for Scientific and Technological Affairs at the US Embassy in Tokyo, 7 August 1987.
21. *Asahi Shimbun* (evening edition), 10 August 1987.
22. *Asahi Shimbun* (evening edition), 10 August 1987.
23. *Asahi Shimbun*, 8 February 1988.
24. *Asahi Shimbun*, 23 December 1982.
25. For details on Japan's role in the US Far Eastern nuclear operations since the 1950s, see Peter Hayes, Lyuba Zarsky and Walden Bello, *American Lake: Nuclear Peril in the Pacific*, Harmondsworth, Middx: Penguin (1987).

26. Reinhard Drifte, in Chapman, Drifte and Gow, op. cit., p. 121.
27. Kosaka Masataka, 'Theater nuclear weapons and Japan's defense policy', in Richard H. Solomon and Kosaka Masataka (eds), *The Soviet Far East Military Buildup: Nuclear Dilemmas and Asian Security*, London: Croom Helm (1986), p. 135.
28. *Asahi Evening News*, 28 November 1985.
29. Reinhard Drifte, in Chapman, Drifte and Gow, op. cit., p. 122.
30. *Daily Yomiuri*, 23 December 1981; *Mainichi Daily News*, 19–20 May 1981.
31. David C. Morrison, 'Defense focus', *National Journal*, 25 April 1987, p. 1036.
32. *Asahi Shimbun*, 16 April 1987.
33. *Korea Herald*, 23 August 1987.
34. *Newsletter for a Nuclear Free Japan and Pacific-Asia (Tokyo)*, 2 (March 1986); *Asahi Shimbun*, 6 August 1987.
35. *Daily Yomiuri*, 27 November 1984.
36. Reinhard Drifte, in Chapman, Drifte and Gow, op. cit., p. 122.
37. J. Frankel, 'Domestic politics of Japan's foreign policy', *International Studies*, 3, 158.
38. Imai Ryukichi, '*Nihon kaku busoron ni tsuite: jungi jut suron kara mo Nihon was kakubuso dekinu*', *Asahi Janaru*, 15 September 1975, pp. 10–15.
39. For a detailed discussion of Japan's nuclear option, see John E. Endicott, *Japan's Option: Political Technical and Strategic Factors*, New York: Praeger (1975).

Chapter III

1. Reinhard Drifte, in J. W. M. Chapman, R. Drifte and I. T. M. Gow, *Japan's Quest for Comprehensive Security: Defence–Diplomacy–Dependence*, London: Frances Pinter (1983), pp. 128ff.
2. Eisenhower Library, Folder: Conference Staff coverage (5) Box 1.
3. Ibid.

4. *Atoms in Japan*, July 1988, p. 22.
5. *'87 Genshiryoku Nenkan (1987 Nuclear Energy Yearbook)*, Tokyo: Nihon Genshiryoku Sangyo Kaigi (1987), p. 51.
6. *Atoms in Japan*, July 1988, p. 25.
7. *Atoms in Japan*, 13, 2 (February 1987), pp. 33ff. See also, *Long-Term Program for Development and Utilization of Nuclear Energy*, 22 June 1987, Atomic Energy Commission, and *'87 Genshiryoku Nenkan*, op. cit., pp. 167ff.
8. *NUKEM Special Report: Japan*, January 1987, Hanau, p. 30; A.Y. Shoda, 'The present status and prospects of nuclear power generation in Japan', *Asien*, 24 (July 1987), 59; *Atoms in Japan*, August 1988, p. 4.
9. *'87 Genshiryoku Nenkan*, op. cit., p. 133; *NUKEM Special Report: Japan*, January 1987, Hanau, p. 21.
10. The *Nihon Genshiryoku Sangyokai* (Japanese Nuclear Power Industrial Forum) mentions in its yearbook 1987 (op. cit., p. 123) the year 2030 for the FBR becoming operational.
11. *NUKEM Special Report: Japan*, January 1987, Hanau, p. 37.
12. *NUKEM Special Report: Japan*, January 1987, Hanau, p. 35; *Atoms in Japan*, 31, 1 (January 1987), 13–14.
13. *Daily Yomiuri*, 19 June 1987 (reprint of an article by Timothy Appel from the *Christian Science Monitor*): *Daily Yomiuri*, 16 December 1987. See the opinion expressed by two Democrat members of the Foreign Affairs Committee of the House of Representatives opposing the argument: *International Herald Tribune*, 2 March 1988.
14. *Nuclear Fuel*, 27 July 1987, p. 13.
15. Letter from the NRC to President Reagan, 27 July 1987.
16. *Asahi Evenings News*, 12 March 1983.
17. *Asahi Shimbun*, 14 April 1987.
18. Reinhard Drifte, 'China', in Jozef Goldblat (ed.), *Non-Proliferation: The Why and the Wherefore*, London: Taylor & Francis/ SIPRI (1985), pp. 45–55.
19. *Atoms in Japan*, 29, 7 (July 1985).
20. *International Herald Tribune*, 25 September 1985.
21. Lewis A. Dunn, 'The view from the US', *Journal of North-East Asian Studies*, 5, 4 (winter 1986), 10.
22. *Asian Defence Journal*, October 1987, p. 132.

94   *Japan's rise to international responsibilities*

23. *Le Monde*, 10 April 1980; *Japan Times*, 2 September 1981.
24. For a discussion of this approach to arms control, see John H. Barton and Imai Ryukichi (eds), *Arms Control II: A New Approach to International Security*, Cambridge, Mass.: Oelgeschlager, Gunn & Hain (1981), and Janne E. Nolan, 'US–Soviet conventional arms transfer negotiations', in Alexander George (ed.), *US-Soviet Security Regimes*, Oxford: Oxford University Press (1987).
25. *Financial Times*, 16 December 1987; *Frankfurter Allgemeine Zeitung*, 22 December 1987.
26. *International Herald Tribune*, 20 September 1988.
27. 'Allies to curb flow of missile technology', *Wall Street Journal*, 17 April 1987, p. 8.
28. *Washington Post*, 17 April 1987. For the most detailed account of the guidelines, see Communiqué no. 069 of the Canadian Department of external Affairs of 16 April 1987.
29. Some of this information is based on an interview conducted with a Japanese government official in August 1987 as well as *Nihon Keizai Shimbun*, 1 December 1983.
30. 'Tightening the reins in ballistic missile race', *New York Times*, 19 April 1987.
31. Communiqué of the Canadian Department of External Affairs, op. cit.
32. Interview with a high official of the Japanese Foreign Ministry, 18 August 1987.
33. *Nihon Keizai Shimbun*, 1 December 1983 and 29 January 1987.
34. 'Secrecy long kept in the talks to limit the missile spread', *New York Times*, 17 April 1987.
35. Maeda Hisashi, '*Nihon no tachiba*', in *Asahi Shimbun* (ed.), *Nihon No Anzenhosho*, Tokyo: Asahi Shinbunsha (1967), p. 248.
36. CD/389 of 1983, CD/524 of July 1984 and CD/626 of August 1985.
37. Interview with Miyamoto Yuji, chief of the Disarmament Division, 19 March 1987.
38. Press conference by Matsuda Yoshifumi, Director General for Public Information and Cultural Affairs, Ministry of

Foreign Affairs, 5 February 1987.
39. Imai Ryukichi, 'Arms control and disarmament today: a Japanese view', *Japan Review of International Affairs*, 1, 1 (spring/summer 1987), 32.
40. *Asahi Shimbun*, 12 February 1982.
41. Reinhard Drifte, in Chapman, Drifte and Gow, op. cit. p. 122.
42. '*Kokusai rengo dai 30 kai sokai no jigyo*', Ministry of Foreign Affairs, 1976, p. 259.
43. UN Document A/C. 1/34 PV. 50 (New York), 1979, p. 22.

Chapter IV

1. See also Reinhard Drifte, 'Arms control and the super-power balance in Asia', in Gerald Segal (ed.), *Arms Control in Asia*, London: Macmillan (1987), p. 25.
2. Georges Tan Eng Bok, *The USSR in East Asia*, Paris: Atlantic Institute for International Affairs (1986), p. 75; Ralph Cossa, 'Soviet eyes on Asia', *Air Force Magazine*, August 1985, p. 55.
3. Deliberations of the special Committee on Security of the Lower House Record of 15 July 1981, p. 5. It was also the first time that a ranking government official disclosed that Japan and the US were discussing this issue – *Japan Times Weekly*, 18 July 1981. In November 1981 the government warned against the deployment to Siberia of SS-20 removed from Europe – Radio Japan, 10 November 1981. In January 1982 Japan asked the Soviet Union to remove these missiles from the Far East – *Daily Yomiuri*, 20 February 1982.
4. Speech by Foreign Minister Kuranari to the Annual Conference of the IISS, Kyoto, 8 September 1986. For an expert Japanese view of the differences between European and Japanese perspectives, see John Roper and Yukio Sato, 'European and Japanese public debate over INF modernization: lessons for the future of Western security co-operation', in Richard H. Solomon and Masataka Kosaka (eds), *The Soviet Far East Military Buildup: Nuclear Dilemmas and Asian Security*, London: Croom Helm (1986), pp. 256–70.

5. The author is aware of only two American voices calling for INF deployments in Japan: retired Admiral Zumwalt, quoted in *Süddeutsche Zeitung*, 11 January 1982, and Herbert Schandler who suggested it as an unlikely alternative to bring the Soviets to a deal on SS-20 in Asia – Herbert Y. Schandler, 'US interests and arms control issues in Northeast Asia', presented at the Pacific Symposium, Honolulu, Hawaii, 21 February 1985, pp. 19–20.

6. Reinhard Drifte in J.W.M. Chapman, R. Drifte and I.T.M. Gow, *Japan's Quest for Comprehensive Security: Defence–Diplomacy–Dependence*, London: Frances Pinter (1983), p. 137.

7. *Japan Times*, 21 January 1983.

8. BBC Monitoring Service, SWB SU/7298, 4 April 1983.

9. *Die Zeit*, 31 October 1986, translation by the author.

10. SWB SU/8115/A3/2, 22 November 1985.

11. SWB FE/8160/A2/1, 18 January 1986.

12. *Daily Yomiuri*, 21 May 1987.

13. Interview with Victor Karpov by Christoph Bertram, *Die Zeit*, 11 September 1987, translation by the author.

14. *Asahi Shimbun*, 8 January 1986; *Yomiuri Shimbun*, 18 February 1986.

15. *Daily Yomiuri*, 7 October 1986.

16. *Tokyo Shimbun*, 4 March 1987; *Daily Yomiuri*, 9 June 1987.

17. *Kyodo*, 7 November 1986; FBIS-APA 86-216, 7 November 1986, IV, 216, Daily Report Asia & Pacific.

18. *Daily Yomiuri*, 22 September 1987.

19. *Daily Yomiuri*, 30 April 1987.

20. *Daily Yomiuri*, 5 March 1987.

21. *Daily Yomiuri*, 17 December 1987; *Korea Herald*, 16 December 1987.

22. *Der Spiegel*, 3 June 1985, p. 16; *Neue Zürcher Zeitung*, 21 January 1986.

23. *Frankfurter Allgemeine Zeitung*, 16 May 1987.

24. *International Herald Tribune*, 20 May 1987; *Daily Yomiuri*, 21 May 1987.

25. *International Herald Tribune*, 2 July and 23 July 1987.

26. Mikhail Gorbachev's interview with the newspaper *Merdeka*, Novosti Press Agency press release (London), 23

July 1987, pp. 6–7.
27. Ibid., p.5.
28. The author received from Takahashi Minoru, the journalist who conducted the interview in Moscow on 12 August 1987, a copy of his Japanese report on the interview. Earlier, however, a Soviet embassy official in Tokyo declared that American nuclear arms allegedly deployed in Japan were not linked to the Soviet INF agreement. *Kyodo* in English, 24 July 1987; FBIS-EAS Northeast Asia, 24 July 1987, p. A1. For the text of the Gorbachev interview in *Merdeka*, see Novisti Press Agency press release, 23 July 1987.
29. *International Herald Tribune*, 24 July 1987. The goodwill characterized by the removal of Asian INF was also stressed by Soviet Vice-Foreign Minister Anatoly Adamishin in December 1987 – *Daily Yomiuri*, 17 December 1987.
30. *Asahi Shimbun*, 10 December 1987. The intrusion was probably because of a navigational error, as the aircraft later landed in North Korea which is unusual for this kind of reconnaissance flight over Japan. *Daily Yomiuri*, 17 December 1987.

Chapter V

1. Kimura Hiroshi, 'Arms control in Asia', in Adam M. Garfinkle (ed.), *Global Perspectives on Arms Control*, New York: Praeger (1984), p. 91.
2. For a discussion of the inherent instabilities of the maritime strategy, see Andrew Mack, *Arms Control in the North Pacific*, Working Paper No. 36, Australian University, Canberra, March 1988, pp. 23ff.
3. Hasegawa Tsuyoshi, 'Soviet arms control policy in Asia and the US-Japan alliance', *Japan Review of International Affairs*, 2, 2 (fall/winter 1988), 206.
4. Paul G. Johnston, 'Tomahawk: the implications of a strategic/tactical mix', *Proceedings of the Naval Academy*, April 1982, pp, 26–33; Russell S. Hibbs, 'An uncontrollable Tomahawk?', *Proceedings of the Naval Academy*, January 1985,

pp. 66–70; Tom Stefanick, 'America's maritime strategy – the arms control implications', *Arms Cotnrol Today*, December 1986, pp. 10–17.

5.   *Washington Post*, 29 November 1986.

6.   Desmond Ball, 'Nuclear war at sea', *International Security*, winter 1985/86, pp. 3–31.

7.   *Jane's Defence Weekly*, 14 March 1987, p. 416.

8.   *International Herald Tribune*, 22 May 1987.

9.   Robert O'Neill, 'The balance of naval power in the Pacific: implications for force structure', special exposition supplement ENSA/NAVTEC '86, *Pacific Defence Reporter* 1986.

10. One of the earliest discussions of CBM in Asia is in John H. Barton and Ryukichi Imai (eds) *Arms Control II: A New Approach to International Security*, Cambridge, Mass: Oelgeschlager, Gunn & Hain (1981).

11. 'Confidence building measures', report of the UN Secretary General (A/34/416), p. 3; 'Comprehensive study on confidence building measures', report of the Secretary General (A/36/474), New York: United Nations (1982), p. 2. For the global application of CBM, see also Jonathan Alford (ed.), *The Future of Arms Control, Part III: Confidence Building Measures*, London: IISS (1979).

12. 'Study on the naval arms race', report of the UN Secretary General, A/40/535, 17 September 1985, published as *UNDisarmament Study Series*, 16 (1986), 75–6.

13. Reinhard Drifte, 'Arms control and the superpower balance in Asia', in Gerald Segal (ed.), *Arms Control in Asia*, London: Macmillan (1987), p. 32. For full text of Soviet proposal, see CD/498, 16 April 1984.

14. Reinhard Drifte, 'Arms control and the superpower balance in Asia', op. cit., p. 33. See also Kimura Hiroshi, 'The Soviet proposal of confidence building measures', *Journal of International Affairs*, summer 1983, p. 86 (reprinted as *Japan's New World Role*, edited by Joshua D. Katz and Tilly Friedman-Lichtschein, Boulder, Colo.: Westview Press (1985).

15. Mikhail Gorbachev's interview with the newspaper *Merdeka*, Novosti Press Agency press release (London), 23 July 1987, p. 7.

16. Mikhail Gorbachev, 'Time for actions, time for practical work', speech in Krasnoyarsk, 16 September 1988, Novosti Press Publishing House, Moscow (1988), pp. 25–6.
17. *Far Eastern economic Review*, 12 January 1989.
18. Kimura Hiroshi, 'Gorbachev's foreign policy in Asia and the Pacific', *Japan Review of International Affairs* 1, 1 (spring/summer 1987), 87.
19. For a detailed discussion of the official point of view, see Kimura Hiroshi, 'The Soviet proposal of confidence building measures', op. cit., pp. 81–104.
20. See, e.g., Secretary of Defense Weinberger's speech in Anchorage: 'Not satisfied with the massive strategic imbalance in their favor, the Soviets call for regional arms control talks to discuss limits and restrictions on our naval forces and overseas basing in the region. That, of course, is the Soviet propaganda ploy that attempts to paint American forces as the threat to regional security', Anchorage World Affairs Council, 7 October 1986, Department of Defense news release.
21. BBC, SWB FE/7959/A2/1, 24 May 1985. See also Nakasone's meeting with Honecker in East Berlin in January 1987 – *Daily Yomiuri*, 15 January 1987. Also Foreign Minister Kuranari during his visit to Bangladesh, SWP FE/8501/i, 25 February 1987.
22. *Far Eastern economic Review*, 29 December 1989.
23. For detailed and pragmatic proposals for naval arms control in the North Pacific, see conference attribution by Barry M. Blechman at a conference on security and arms control in the North Pacific, Camberra, August 1987 (proceedings to be published), as well as John Borawski, 'Risk reduction at sea: naval confidence building measures', *Naval Forces*, 1987, pp. 18–28.
24. Reinhard Drifte, 'Arms control and the superpower balance in Asia', op. cit., p. 34.
25. *Far Eastern economic Review*, 9 January 1986, p. 13; *Nihon Keizai Shimbun*, 26 October 1986, p. 2.
26. Quoted in Kimura Hiroshi, op. cit., p. 88.
27. *Daily Yomiuri*, 16 December 1988.

28. *Japan Times*, 9 October 1985; *International Herald Tribune*, 8 November 1985.
29. For a very detailed analysis of the Korean tinderbox, see Edward A. Olsen, 'The arms race on the Korean peninsula', *Asian Survey*, 26, 8 (August 1986).
30. Reinhard Drifte, 'Arms control and the superpower balance in Asia', op. cit., p. 36.
31. For details, see Reinhard Drifte, 'Arms control and the superpower balance in Asia', op. cit., pp. 34ff.
32. Interview with US State Department official in 1986 concerning US invitations to North Korean observers to Team Spirit manoeuvres. The author was told that it did not even occur to the Administration to get public support for this from the Japanese government. See also the exchange between Congressman Solarz and John Monjo, Deputy Assistant Secretary of State, quoted in Reinhard Drifte, 'Arms control and the superpower balance in Asia', op. cit., p. 37.
33. *International Herald Tribune*, 4–5 April 1987.
34. Ahn Byung-joon, 'Arms control proposals of North and South Korea and their implications for Korean security', *Korean Journal of International Relations*, 26, 2 (1986), 147.
35. *Korea Herald*, 21 and 27 February 1988.
36. Professor Iwashima presented his ideas in the following articles: '*Nihon no atarashii mishi:* positive pacifism (Japan's new way: Positive pacifism)', *Keizai Fukko*, 1457 (June 1987), 5–14; '*Hitsuyo na "Shinrai kosei" no noryoku* (Efforts for confidence building)', *Manichi Shimbun*, 10 December 1987; '*Masatsu kaisho no atarashii michi* (A new way to resolve frictions)', *Tokyo Shimbun* (evening edition), 9 July 1987; conference paper, 1 June 1987, 'On the issue of Korean unification', organized by the *Kantai Heiyo Mondai Kenkyusho*, Tokyo.
37. Sakamoto Yoshikazu, *Sekai*, January 1983.
38. Nakamura Yoshihisa, '*Shinrai sosei setchi to Nihon no yokuseiryoku*', in Nakamura Yoshihisa (ed.), *Shinsedai No Senryaku Shiso (Strategic thinking in the New Era)*, Tokyo (1987), pp. 21–2; see also Nakamura Yoshihisa, '*Shinrai sosei sechi to boei seisaku*', op. cit., p. 13.
39. Yamamoto Takehiko, '*Hokuto ajia ni okeruy gunbi kanri*

(Arms control in East Asia)', in Shindo Eiichi (ed.), *Heiwa Senryaku No Kozu* (*The Design for Peace Strategy*), Tokyo: Nihon Hyoronsha (1986), pp. 89–121.

Chapter VI

1. See, e.g., Ambassador Imai on 13 February 1986, CD/PV, 339, p. 18, or, speaking in a much more direct way, Ambassador Yamada, 10 February 1987, CD/PV. 387, p. 10.
2. 'The application of (nuclear) safeguards remote verification technology to verify the chemical weapons convention', Working Paper CD/619, July 1985.
3. 'Verification of non-production under the Chemical Weapons Convention', CD/CW/WP, 174, 30 July 1987.
4. See, e.g., the editorial in the *Daily Yomiuri*, 9 September 1987.
5. *International Herald Tribune*, 5 May 1988.
6. *Jane's Defence Weekly*, 9 August 1986.
7. *International Herald Tribune*, 17–18 september 1988.
8. CD/PV, 291, p. 14, 14 February 1985.

Chapter VII

1. Imai Ryukichi, 'Arms control and disarmament today: a Japanese view', *Japan Review of International Affairs*, 1, 1 (spring/summer 1987), 25–40.
2. Conference on 'Global peace and regional security', Tokyo, 29 October 1982.
3. Adlai Stevenson, 'International aspects of technology development and transfer', in *Comprehensive Security: Japanese and US Perspectives*, a special report of the Northeast Asia-United States Forum on International Policy, Stanford (1981), pp. 113–20.
4. Iwashima Iwao, '*Nihon no atarashii michi*: positive pacifism (Japan's new way: positive pacifism)', *Keizai Fukko*, 1457 (June 1987), 5–14.
5. Imai Ruykichi, '*Diplomatie und Rüstungskontrolle: Zur Beteiligung von Drittstaaten an de Überwachung von Rüs-*

tungskontrollabkommen', (original English draft title 'Compliance diplomacy and modern arms control: problems of third party participation'), *Europa Archiv.*, 11 (10 June 1985).

6. Imai, ibid. The importance of access to technical information is also stressed in his 'Arms control and disarmament today: a Japanese view', op. cit., p. 39.

7   *Japan Times*, 31 January 1985, the quote here is based on the original Diet record (*Shugiinkaigiroku*, 8 (19 January 1985), 296). See also Nakasone's intervention on the Diet's Budget Committee on 21 February 1985, *Yosaniinkaigijiroku*, 15 (21 February 1985), 27.

8. *Daily Yomiuri*, 22 February 1985. My reference is based on the original Diet record, *Yosaniinkaigijiroki*, 15 (21 February 1985), 27.

9. Imai Ryukichi, 'Diplomatie und Rüstungskontrolle', op. cit.

10. *International Herald Tribune*, 17 September 1987.

Chapter VIII

1. Richard L. Armitage, 'US security role in East Asia', *Defense Issues*, 3, 11, Department of Defense.

2. Hasegawa Tsuyoshi, 'Soviet arms control policy in Asia and the US-Japan alliance', *Japan review of International Affairs*, 2, 2 (fall/winter 1988), 206.

Bibliography

Books:

Alford, Jonathan (ed.), *The Future of Arms Control, Part III: Confidence Building Measures* (1979).

Barton, John H. and Imai, Ryukichi, *Arms Control II: A New Approach to International Security* (1981).

Bull, Hedley, *The Control of the Arms Race* (1961).

Buzan, Barry, *An Introduction to Strategic Studies, Military Technology and International Relations* (1987).

Chapman, J.W.M., Drifte, Reinhard and Gow, Ian, *Japan's Quest for Comprehensive Security: Defence-Diplomacy-Dependence* (1983).

Drifte, Reinhard, *Arms Production in Japan* (1986)

Drifte, Reinhard, 'China', in Joseph Goldblat (ed.). *Non-Proliferation: The Why and the Wherefore* (1985).

Drifte, Reinhard, 'Arms control and the superpower balance in Asia, in *Arms Control in Asia* Gerald Segal (ed.), (1987).

Endicott, John E., *Japan's Option: Political, Technical and Strategic Factors* (1975).

Georges Tan Eng Bok, *The USSR in East Asia* (1986).

Hayes, Peter, Lyuba, Zarsky and Walden, Bello, *American Lake: Nuclear Peril in the Pacific* (1987).

Katz, Joshua D. and Friedman-Lichtschein, Tilly (eds.). *Japan's*

New World Role (1985).

Kimura, Hiroshi, 'Arms control in Asia', in Adam M. Garfinkle (ed.), *Global Perspectives on Arms Control*, (1984).

Mack, Andrew, *Arms Control in the North Pacific,* Working Paper no. 36 (1988).

Maeda, Hisashi, 'Nihon no tachiba', in *Asahi Shimbun*, (ed.), *Nihon No Anzenhosho* (1967).

Nakamura, Yoshihisa (ed.), *Shinsedai Wo Senryaku Shiso (Strategic Thinking in the New Era)* (1987).

Nolan, Janne E. and George, Alexander (eds.), 'US-Soviet conventional arms transfer negotiations, in *US-Soviet Security Regimes* (1987).

Solomon, Richard H. and Kosaka, Masataka (eds.), *The Soviet Far East Military Buildup: Nuclear Dilemmas and Asian Security* (1986).

Stevenson, Adlai, 'International aspects of technology development and transfer in: *Comprehensive Security: Japanese and US Perspectives* a special report of the Northeast-Asia–United States Forum on International Policy, Stanford (1981).

Yamamoto Takehiko, 'Hokuto Ajia ni okeru gunbi knari (Arms control in East Asia)', in Shindo Eiichi (ed.), *Heiwa Senryaku No Kozu (The Design for 'Peace Strategy)* (1986).

'87 Genshiryoku Nenkan (1987 Nuclear Energy Yearbook) (1987).

Articles

Ball, Desmond, 'Nuclear war at sea', *International Security*, winter 1985/1986, 3–31.

Cossa, Ralph, 'Soviet eyes on Asia', *Air Force Magazine*, August 1985.

Dunn, A. Lewis, 'The view from the US', *Journal of Northeast Asian Studies*, V, 4 (winter 1986).

Frankel, J., 'Domestic politics of Japan's foreign policy', *International Studies*, 3.

Hasegawa, Tsuyoshi, 'Soviet arms control policy in Asia and the US-Japan alliance', *Japan Review of International Affairs*, 2, 2, (fall/winter 1988).

Hibbs, S. Russell, 'An uncontrollable Tomahawk?', *Proceedings of the Naval Academy*, January 1985, 66–70.

Imai Ryukichi, 'Science, technology and diplomacy: a case study on Japan', Working paper for the 4 March 1987 meeting of the Study Group on Technological Change and Foreign Policy, Council on Foreign Relations, New York.

Imai, Ryukichi, '*Nihon kaku busoron ni tsuite* (On the non-nuclear status of Japan)', *Asahi Janaru* 15 September 1975, 10–15.

Imai, Ryukichi, 'Arms control and disarmament today: a Japanese view', *Japan Review of International Affairs*, 1, 1 (spring/summer 1987), 25–40.

Imai, Ryukichi, '*Diplomatie und Rüstungskontrolle: Zur Beteiligung von Drittstaaten an der Überwachung von Rüstungskontrollabkommen*' (original English draft title 'Compliance diplomacy and modern arms control: problems of Third Party participation'), *Europa Archiv*, 11 (10 June 1985).

Iwashima, Iwao, '*Nihon no atarashii michi*: positive pacifism (Japan's new way: positive pacifism)', *Keizai Fukko*, 1457 (June 1987), 5–14.

Johnston, Paul G., 'Tomahawk: the implications of a strategic/tactical mix', *Proceedings of the Naval Academy*, April 1982, 26–33.

Kimura, Hiroshi, 'The Soviet proposal of confidence-building measures', *Journal of International Affairs*, summer 1983, 86 (reprint as *Japan's New World Role*, edited by Joshua D. Katz and Tilly Friedman-Lichtschein (1985).

Kimura, Hiroshi, 'Gorbachev's foreign policy in Asia and the Pacific', *Japan Review of International Affairs*, 1, 1 (spring/summer 1987).

Morrison, David C., 'Defense focus', *National Journal*, 25 April 1987.

Nakamura, Yoshihisa, '*Shinrai josei sotchi to Nihon no yokushiryoku*, CBM and Japan's deterrence capability', *Kokubo*, October 1986, 8–24.

Olsen,, Edward A., 'The arms race on the Korean peninsula', *Asian Survey*, 26, 8 (August 1986).

O'Neill, Robert, 'The balance of naval power in the Pacific: implications for force structure', special exposition supplement ENSA/NAVTEC '86, *Pacific Defence Reporter 1986*.

Sakamoto, Yoshikazu, *Sekai*, January 1983.
Schandler, Herbert Y., 'US interests and arms control issues in Northeast Asia', presented at the Pacific Symposium, Honolulu, Hawaii, 21 February 1985, p. 19–20.
Stefanick, Tom, 'America's maritime strategy – the arms control implications', *Arms Control Today*, December 1986, 10–17.

Primary Resources

Richard L. Armitage, 'US security role in East Asia', *Defense Issues*, 11, Department of Defense.
Communiqué no. 069 of the Canadian Department of External Affairs of 16 April 1987.
Deliberations of the Special Committee on Security of the Lower House Record of 15 July 1981 (in Japanese).
Budget Committee on 21 February 1985, *Yosaniinkaigijiroku*, 15, 21 February 1985 (in Japanese).
Mikhail Gorbachev's interview with the newspaper *Merdeka*, Novosti Press Agency press release (London, 23 July 1987.
Mikhail Gorbachev, 'Time for actions, time for practical work', speech in Krasnoyarsk, 16 September 1988, Novosti Press Agency Publishing House, Moscow (1988).
'Japan's contribution to military stability in Northeast Asia', prepared for the Subcommittee on East Asian and Pacific Affairs of the Committee on Foreign Relations, United States Senate, by the US Arms Control and Disarmament Agency, Washington, June 1980, 77 pp.
Imai Ryukichi, 17 April 1984, Committee on Disarmament, CD/PV. 259.
CD/389 of 1983, CD/524 of July 1984 and CD/626 of August 1985.
14 February 1985, CD/PV. 291.
'The application of (nuclear) safeguards remote verification technology to verify the chemical weapons convention', Working Paper CD/619, July 1985.

'Verification of non-production under the Chemical Weapons Convention', CD/CW/WP. 174, 30 July 1987.

Ambassador Imai on 13 February 1986, CD/PV. 339.

Ambassador Yamada on 10 February 1987, CD/PV. 387.

Kuranari, Tadashi, 'Japan-US relationship: to further strengthen the partnership between the two countries', 19 April 1987 (Ministry of Foreign Affairs, Tokyo).

Speech by Foreign Minister Kuranari to the Annual Conference of the IISS, Kyoto, 8 September 1986.

UN Document A/C. 1/34 PV. 50, New York, 1979.

'Confidence-building measures', report of the Secretary General (A/34/416), New York (United Nations).

'Comprehensive study on confidence-building measures', report of the Secretary General (A/36/474), New York (United Nations) 1982.

'Study on the naval arms race', report of the UN Secretary General, A/40/535, 17 September 1985, published as *UN Disarmament Study Series*, 16 (1986).

'World military expenditures and arms transfers 1986', Arms Control and Disarmament Agency (ACDA), Washington, 1987.

'Defense of Japan 1985', Defense Agency, Tokyo, 1985.

Eisenhower Library, Folder: Conferences-Staff coverage (5) Box 1.

'NUKEM Special Report: Japan', January 1987, Hanau, p. 30.

Newspapers

Asahi Evening News, 17 April 1984.

Asahi Shimbun (evening edition), 8 April 1987 and 10 April 1987.

Asahi Shimbun, 6 August 1987.

Asahi Shimbun (evening edition), 10 August 1987.

Asahi Shimbun, 8 February 1988.

Asahi Shimbun, 23 December 1982.

Asahi Evening News, 28 November 1985.

Asahi Shimbun, 16 April 1987.
Asahi Shimbun, 8 January 1986.
Asahi Shimbun, 10 December 1987.

Atoms in Japan, 29, 7, July 1985.
Atoms in Japan, 31, 2, February 1987.
Atoms in Japan, July 1988.
Atoms in Japan, August 1988.

BBC Monitoring Service SWB SU/7298, 4 April 1983.
BBC SWB FE/7959/A2/1, 24 May 1985.

The *Daily Yomiuri*, 23 December 1981.
The *Daily Yomiuri*, 4 January 1984.
The *Daily Yomiuri*, 27 November 1984.
The *Daily Yomiuri*, 22 February 1985.
The *Daily Yomiuri*, 7 October 1986.
The *Daily Yomiuri*, 5 March 1987.
The *Daily Yomiuri*, 30 April 1987.
The *Daily Yomiuri*, 21 May 1987.
The *Daily Yomiuri*, 9 June 1987.
The *Daily Yomiuri*, 19 June 1987.
The *Daily Yomiuri*, 22 September 1987.
The *Daily Yomiuri*, 16 December 1987.
The *Daily Yomiuri*, 17 December 1987.
The *Daily Yomiuri*, 16 December 1988.

Die Zeit, 31 October 1986.
Die Zeit, 11 September 1987.

Far Eastern Economic Review, 27 August 1987.
Far Eastern Economic Review, 25 September 1986.
Far Eastern Economic Review, 12 January 1989.
Far Eastern Economic Review, 29 December 1989.

Frankfurter Allgemeine Zeitung, 16 May 1987.
Frankfurter Allgemeine Zeitung, 22 December 1987.

FBIS-APA-86-216, 7 November 1986, IV, 216, Daily Report Asia & Pacific.

Financial Times, 16 December 1987.

International Herald Tribune, 4–5 April 1987.
International Herald Tribune, 13 April 1987.
International Herald Tribune, 20 May 1987.
International Herald Tribune, 5 November 1987.
International Herald Tribune, 2 March 1988.
International Herald Tribune, 17–18 September 1988.
International Herald Tribune, 20 September 1988.

Jane's Defence Weekly, 2 November 1985.
Jane's Defence Weekly, 14 March 1987.

Japan Times Weekly, 18 July 1981.
Japan Times, 2 September 1981.
Japan Times, 21 January 1983.

Journal of Japanese Trade & Industry, 3 (1987).

Korea Herald, 8–9 June 1987.
Korea Herald, 23 August 1987.
Korea Herald, 16 December 1987.
Korea Herald, 21 and 27 February 1988.

Kyodo in English, 10 September 1985.
Kyodo, 7 November 1986.
Kyodo in English, 24 July 1987, FBIS-EAS Northeast Asia, 24 July 1987 p. A1.

Mainichi Daily News, 19–20 May 1981.
Mainichi Shimbun 10 December 1987.

Le Monde, 10 April 1980.

Neue Zürcher Zeitung, 21 January 1986.

Newsletter for a Nuclear Free Japan and Pacific-Asia (Tokyo), 2 (March 1986).

The *New York Times*, 25 November 1986.
The *New York Times*, 17 April 1987.
The *New York Times*, 19 April 1987.

Nihon Keizai Shimbun, 1 December 1983.
Nihon Keizai Shimbun, 23 March 1986.
Nihon Keizai Shimbun, 26 October 1986.
Nihon Keizai Shimbun, 29 January 1987.
Nihon Keizai Shimbun, 26 July 1987.

Der Spiegel, 3 June 1985.

Süddeutsche Zeitung, 11 January 1982.

SWB SU/8115/A3/2, 22 November 1985.
SWB FE/8160/A2/1, 18 January 1986.

Tokyo Shimbun, 4 March 1987.
Tokyo Shimbun (evening edition), 9 July 1987.

The *Wall Street Journal*, 17 April 1987.

The *Washington Post*, 29 November 1986.
The *Washington Post*, 17 April 1987.

Yomiuri Shimbun, 18 February 1986.

Index